Five Nights at Freddy's™

COOKBOOK

ISBN 978-1-338-85129-8

10 9 8 7 6 5 4 3 2 23 24 25 26 27

Printed in China 62

First Printing 2023

Amazing15, Project Management and Design
Rob Morris, Writer, Photographer, and Food Stylist
Livia Abraham, Food Stylist
Kevin Pettman, Additional Writing
Rachel Prater, Production Editor, Scholastic
Michael Petranek, Editorial Director AFK & Graphix Media, Scholastic
Jeff Shake, Senior Designer, Scholastic
Yaffa Jaskoll, Creative Director, Scholastic
Special Thanks, Rebecca Woods

Five Nights at Freddy's™

COOKBOOK

By Rob Morris

Scholastic inc.

Contents

MEET THE GANG

Freddy Fazbear

Chica

Foxy

Bonnie

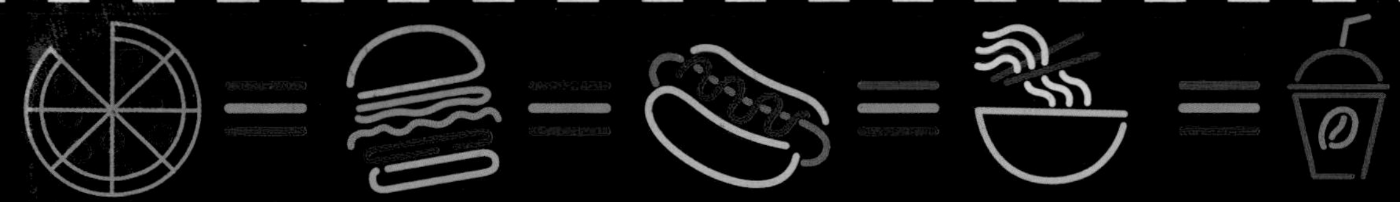

Glamrock Freddy
Glamrock Chica
Roxanne Wolf
Montgomery Gator

BURGERS
& SHAKES

Get Ready for FREDDY'S FOOD!

Are you feeling horridly hungry? In need of lip-licking inspiration to serve the perfect plate tonight? Don't frighten yourself with such foody thoughts, because Freddy Fazbear is here with a huge helping of delicious dishes to keep your belly seriously stuffed!

Friends, family, and visitors to your Pizzaplex (or perhaps just your kitchen, if for some reason you don't do your cooking in an entertainment complex of arcade games and rides) will love the Freddy-themed recipes inside this mouthwatering guide. From all you need to have and know for creating perfect pizzas with tasty toppings to delightful burgers, meaty treats, classic sharing dishes, and something sweet to follow, your *Five Nights at Freddy's* cookbook has it covered. Looking for "not meat" dishes? There's plenty of those, too.

The pages are action packed and take you on a cooking crash course through the fun, and potential pitfalls, of Freddy Fazbear's Mega Pizzaplex. You'll meet lots of interesting animatronic characters along the way, including Roxanne, Chica, and Monty, and discover what's lurking on their menu. Whether you're a full-on Freddy fanatic or a first-time visitor to the Pizzaplex, you're guaranteed to enjoy the mega meals, super snacks, and drinks that'll make you drool. Actually, is it wise to drool over your food? Probably doesn't help the flavor, so best not.

It's time to serve a plate to make Freddy proud!

LOCAL NEWS

Local pizzeria threatened with shutdown over sanitation.

Local pizzeria Freddy Fazbear's Pizza has been threatened again with shutdown by the health department over reports of foul odor coming from the much-loved animal mascots. Police were contacted when parents reportedly noticed what appeared to be blood and mucus [...] the eyes and mouths of the mascots. One [...] them to "reanimated carcasses."

Your Guide to the MEGA PIZZAPLEX

PIZZAPLEX PARTY!

The Pizzaplex, or Freddy Fazbear's Mega Pizzaplex as it is officially known, is a triple-level complex full of adventure. More than just a place to grab a bite to eat and relax in your dining chair, it's a central hub acting as an entertainment zone with plenty to keep guests busy.

Fazer Blast

Roxy Raceway

Monty's Gator Golf

Between your mouthfuls of lovely pizza and whatever else you sumptuously select from the offerings around the Pizzaplex, you should also know the various attractions here. There's the Fazcade arcade center, Bonnie Bowl bowling alley (visitors with a sweet tooth shouldn't miss the ice-cream parlor), and the Fazer Blast laser tag arena. Monty's Gator Golf and the Roxy Raceway are just a couple of other cool areas to explore. The Pizzaplex can be a tough place to survive—please avoid Vanessa the security guard—but with a hearty dish inside you helping to fuel your efforts, there's always hope.

Freddy Fact

In the Faz-Pad restaurant, gorgeous dishes on the menu include Freddy fried rice, pineapple and shrimp tempura, and korma chunks. Fried Brussels sprouts? No thanks!

MISSING CHILDREN

Five children now reported missing. Suspect convicted.

Five children are now linked to the incident at Freddy Fazbear's Pizza, where a man dressed as a cartoon mascot lured them into a back room. While the suspect has been charged, the bodies themselves were never found.
Freddy Fazbear's Pizza has been fighting an uphill battle ever since to convince families to return to the pizzeria."It's a tragedy."

PIZZAPLEX KITCHEN SAFETY

You'll be buzzing more than an animatronic on 10,000 volts to get started on your first day in our kitchens, but this is an important safety alert before you do. These quick kitchen rules are crucial.

Pre-Cooking

1

2 *Wear an apron to protect clothing and tie long hair back.*

3 *Check the recipe list carefully first and make sure you have all the ingredients ready.*

4 *Keep the area where you're cooking clean and tidy.*

During Cooking

5 *If you're not an adult, then you must have one with you to help with sharp knives and operating hot ovens and stoves. Always chop away from yourself when using a blade.*

6 *Protective oven mitts must be used when putting anything in and out of the oven.*

After Cooking

7 *Allow piping-hot food to cool a little before tucking in. Don't rush in as if it's a manic Mazercise fitness session!*

8 *Always clean up after cooking and don't leave hazards around for others to find.*

9 *Once your shift at the Pizzaplex is over, make sure you leave before dark.*

BE CAREFUL!

Sometimes if your food and ingredients are not handled properly, you may become unwell. Always rinse vegetables, fruit, and herbs before using them. Keep raw meat and fish away from other foods. Try to chop raw meat and fish on a separate chopping board, and wash the board and your hands after doing so. Thanks for paying attention to this while working at the Pizzaplex!

100% OF FATAL ACCIDENTS INVOLVE HUMAN BEINGS

Freddy Fazbear's PIZZA

Pizzas are the only place to begin your cooking extravaganza with Freddy Fazbear. As the "front man" of a band, Freddy doesn't mind you adding a touch of glamour to your work in the kitchen to give your pizzas some entertaining twists. Check out the delicious dipping sticks, doughy treats, and cheesy garlic pizza bread in this section, too. Yum!

PIZZAPLEX

MASTER DOUGH

Getting your hands on things and poking stuff is highly recommended around the Pizzaplex, and that's what you need to do when making your dough. Master these essentials and your pizzas will be great every time. Plus, the sauce is just as easy as baiting an animatronic!

MAKES 4 PIZZA BASES

PREPARATION TIME
30 MINUTES

RESTING TIME
1 HOUR

WHAT YOU WILL NEED

Generous 1½ cups/13 fl oz/375 ml lukewarm water

2¼ tsp/¼ oz /7 g dried yeast

1 tsp sugar

3¾ cups/1 lb 2 oz/500 g unbleached bread flour, plus extra for dusting

⅔ cup/3½ oz/100 g fine semolina

1 tsp salt

4 tbsp olive oil, plus extra for greasing

1. In a bowl, mix the warm water, yeast, and sugar together and leave to one side until foamy.
2. Combine the flour, semolina, and salt in a large mixing bowl. Make a well in the center and pour in the foaming yeast liquid and olive oil. Using the handle of a wooden spoon, bring the mixture together to form a dough.
3. Tip the dough onto a lightly floured surface and knead for about 10 minutes until the dough becomes smooth. Brush the inside of a large bowl with olive oil and place the dough in it. Cover with a clean dish towel and leave in a warm place until doubled in size—about an hour should do the trick.
4. Tip the dough onto a lightly floured surface and roll into a log shape. Divide the dough into four even portions. Using a rolling pin, roll the dough out to about 12″ in diameter and top with whatever you like. Cornmeal or fine semolina is great to stretch pizza dough.

THIS IS A WARNING!
The Pizzaplex is not all it seems.
Don't get caught here at night.
The animatronics are coming to life!!!
Be careful out there.

Freddy's Top Tips!

- ★ **There's nothing like making the dough by hand. Yes, it can be a little strenuous, but if you have a food mixer you can let the machine do all the hard work for you.**
- ★ **The dough can be stretched and then frozen to use at a later time, if you wish, or simply frozen as dough balls in plastic bags.**

EASY PLEX PIZZA SAUCE

This sauce will top at least 8 pizzas and can be frozen if you don't use all of it at once.

WHAT YOU WILL NEED

14 oz/400 g can of chopped tomatoes

2 tbsp tomato paste/purée

1 tsp dried oregano

½ tsp sugar

salt and fresh milled pepper to taste

1. Strain the canned tomatoes through a sieve into a bowl, pressing the tomatoes through the mesh with the back of a spoon. Stir in all the other ingredients and there you have it—no cooking required!

Freddy Fazbear's PEPPERONI X-PRESS

A totally tasty treat you can create in next to no time in the Pizzaplex. Freddy fans feel right at home munching on this perfect pepperoni plate, and no doubt Gregory will be lurking nearby looking for a slice of the action, too!

MAKES 2 PIZZAS

PREPARATION TIME
20 MINUTES

COOKING TIME
12–15 MINUTES

WHAT YOU WILL NEED

- All-purpose/plain flour or semolina, for dusting
- 2 balls of Pizzaplex Master Dough (see page 14)
- ½ cup/4¼ oz/120 g Easy Plex Pizza Sauce (see page 15)
- ½ cup/5 oz/140 g grated mozzarella cheese
- 24 slices pepperoni
- 2 tbsp capers (optional)
- Fresh arugula/rocket, to garnish

1. Preheat the oven to 425°F/220°C/gas mark 7. If you are using a pizza stone, put that in the oven to heat up.
2. On a lightly floured surface, roll or stretch out a ball of the dough until it measures roughly 11 inches/28 cm in diameter. Repeat to roll out the other pizza.
3. Spread half the Easy Plex Pizza Sauce over each of the bases, leaving a thin edge bare for the crusts.
4. Sprinkle half the mozzarella cheese over each base. Divide the pepperoni between the pizzas and scatter each with capers.
5. Cook for about 12–15 minutes until the cheese is bubbly and you have a nice golden crust.
6. Cut each pizza into 8 slices and sprinkle arugula leaves on top of each slice.

Freddy Fact

Freddy Fazbear's Mega Pizzaplex has an unusual quick delivery virtual ordering system. If you use this weird piece of food tech, it's a race against time before Chica comes pounding on your door!

PIZZA
FREDDY FAZBEAR

Funtime Foxy's 3-CHEESE VEGGIE SURPRISE

Want to try an appetizing "not meat" pizza? Funtime Foxy is here to help inspire you! Give this fun recipe a go and you're guaranteed to experience a cheesy explosion. Maybe that's the surprise this delicious pizza dish is aiming for?

MAKES 2 PIZZAS

PREPARATION TIME
20 MINUTES

COOKING TIME
12–15 MINUTES

WHAT YOU WILL NEED

All-purpose/plain flour or semolina, for dusting

2 balls Pizzaplex Master Dough (see page 14)

⅔ cup /3½ oz/100 g Easy Plex Pizza Sauce (see page 15)

⅔ cup/2¾ oz/80 g grated mozzarella cheese

⅔ cup/3½ oz/100 g Taleggio cheese

1 jarred roasted red bell pepper, drained and roughly chopped

1 medium zucchini/courgette, thinly sliced

1 tbsp chopped parsley

2 tbsp/⅔ oz/20 g pine nuts

Fresh basil and freshly grated Parmesan cheese, to serve

1. Preheat the oven to 425°F/220°C/gas mark 7. If you are using a pizza stone, put that in the oven to heat up.
2. On a lightly floured surface, roll or stretch out a ball of the dough until it measures roughly 11 inches/28 cm in diameter. Repeat to roll out the other pizza.
3. Spread half the Easy Plex Pizza Sauce over each of the bases, leaving a thin edge bare for the crusts.
4. Sprinkle half the mozzarella over each base, then add little dots of Taleggio to the edge of the crust. Add the chopped bell pepper, sliced zucchini, and chopped parsley. Finally, sprinkle the pine nuts over the top.
5. Bake the pizzas for about 12–15 minutes until the crusts are golden. Just before serving, tear up the basil and add it to the pizza, then grate some Parmesan over the top and enjoy.

Freddy's Top Tips!

★ **For ease, the pizzas are cooked on pizza screens (a metallic, flat, mesh disk). You can usually buy these online from any store that sells kitchenware.**

★ **If you have a pizza stone (a flat slab of ceramic or stone that you place directly on the rack of your oven), put it in the oven for about 30 minutes to heat up. For a crispier crust, put the pizza screen on the stone.**

Freddy's

GARLICKY PIZZA TWIRLS

AND SPICY DIP

The Mega Pizzaplex is full of twists and turns, so get ready for another! Time to step up to the plate with a rockin' recipe for garlicky pizza twirls, along with a chili dipping sauce that's sure to spice up your kitchen.

MAKES 10 TWIRLS

PREPARATION TIME
20 MINUTES

COOKING TIME
10 MINUTES

WHAT YOU WILL NEED

All-purpose/plain flour or semolina, for dusting

1 ball of Pizzaplex Master Dough (see page 14)

2 tbsp/1 oz/30 g butter

3 garlic cloves, crushed

1 tsp chopped fresh parsley

2 tbsp Easy Plex Pizza Sauce (see page 15)

½ cup/1¾ oz/50 g grated mozzarella cheese

1 tbsp finely grated Parmesan cheese

FOR THE DIPPING SAUCE

3 tbsp Easy Plex Pizza Sauce (see page 15)

¼ tsp hot pepper/chili flakes

1 tbsp olive oil

1. Preheat the oven to 425°F/220°C/gas mark 7 and line a baking sheet with parchment paper.
2. On a lightly floured surface, roll the pizza dough to a rough rectangular shape measuring 14 x 8 inches/35 cm x 20 cm.
3. Soften the butter in the microwave, then mix in the crushed garlic and chopped parsley. Brush the garlic butter over the base, right to the edges. Spread the tomato sauce on the base, then sprinkle the mozzarella and Parmesan cheeses on top.
4. Starting from a long edge, roll the dough into a tight cylinder shape. Using a serrated knife, cut the dough into slices about 1¼ inches/3–4 cm thick and place them onto the lined baking sheet with the cut sides facing up. Bake for about 10 minutes until golden.
5. While the dough twirls are cooking, make the dipping sauce by mixing the tomato sauce with the hot pepper flakes and olive oil. Spoon it into a small bowl.
6. Serve the dough twirls with the dipping sauce.

Talking of twists and turns, remember never to turn away and take your eyes off endoskeletons. If you do, they will move and attack!

PIZZA

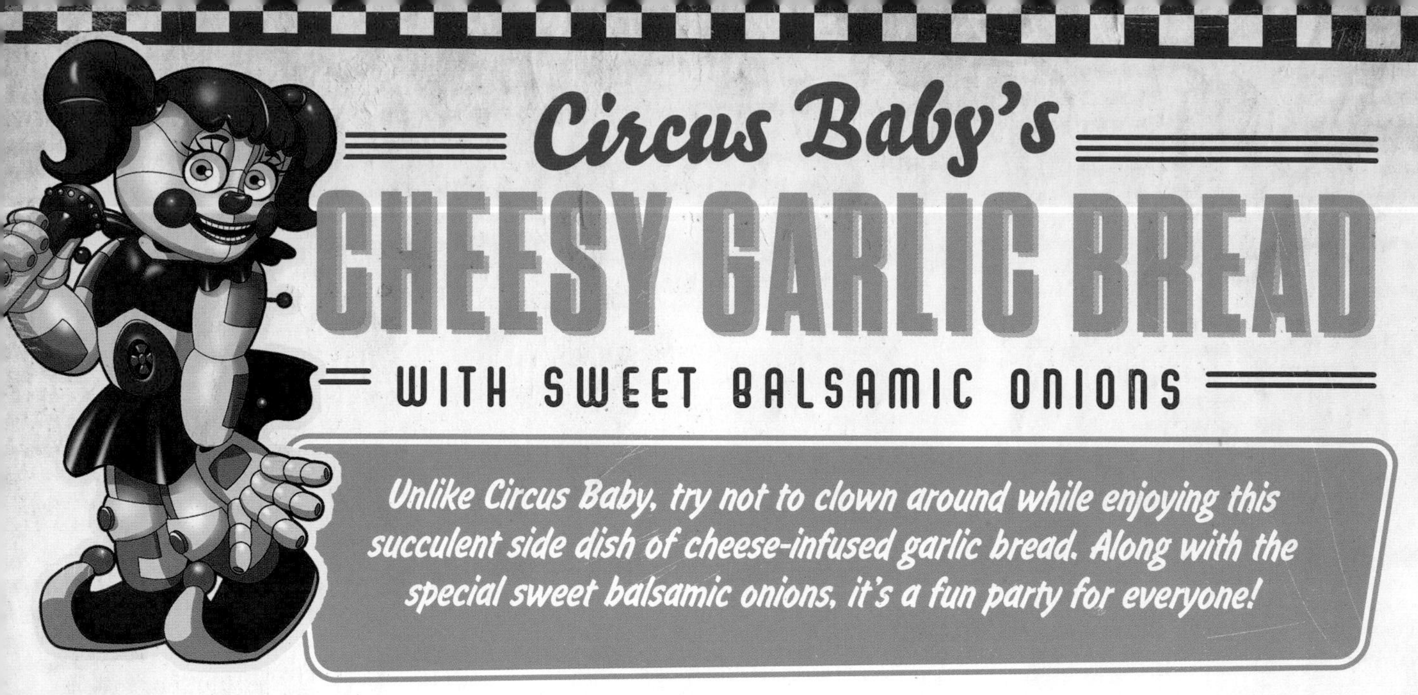

Circus Baby's CHEESY GARLIC BREAD

WITH SWEET BALSAMIC ONIONS

Unlike Circus Baby, try not to clown around while enjoying this succulent side dish of cheese-infused garlic bread. Along with the special sweet balsamic onions, it's a fun party for everyone!

MAKES 4

PREPARATION TIME
20 MINUTES

COOKING TIME
30 MINUTES

WHAT YOU WILL NEED

1 large red onion, sliced
3 tbsp balsamic vinegar
1 tbsp sugar
All-purpose/plain flour or semolina, for dusting
2 balls Pizzaplex Master Dough (see page 14)
3½ tbsp/1¾ oz/50 g butter
4 big garlic cloves, crushed
1 tbsp chopped parsley
Scant 1 cup/3½ oz/100 g grated mozzarella cheese

1. Put the red onion, balsamic vinegar, sugar, and 2 tablespoons of water in a small saucepan and cook over a low heat until the onions are sticky, 10–15 minutes. Remove from the heat and leave to cool. Meanwhile, preheat the oven to 425°F/220°C/gas 7.
2. On a lightly floured surface, divide the dough into four portions and, using a rolling pin, stretch out to whatever shapes you like, making them roughly ¼ inch/½ cm thick. Place onto a pizza screen, if using.
3. Soften the butter in the microwave, then stir in the crushed garlic and chopped parsley. Spread the garlic butter over the pizza bases, leaving a ¾ inch/2 cm crust bare around the edge. Sprinkle the mozzarella cheese on top.
4. Dot the sticky onions over the garlic bread, then place in the oven for about 12 minutes, until the cheese is bubbling and the crust is golden. Slice and eat while they are hot.

Fazbear's DUNKING CINNAMON STICKS *with chocolate sauce*

Sunnydrop Energizing Candy is well known in the Pizzaplex, but cinnamon sticks and chocolate sauce? Not so much! That said, it's always good to try new things, so get going and create this delicious dunking delight.

MAKES 10

PREPARATION TIME
20 MINUTES

COOKING TIME
12 MINUTES

WHAT YOU WILL NEED

All-purpose/plain flour, for dusting

1 ball of Pizzaplex Master Dough (see page 14)

2 tbsp/1 oz/25 g butter, melted

2½ tbsp/1 oz/25 g superfine/caster sugar

1 tsp ground cinnamon

FOR THE CHOCOLATE SAUCE

¼ cup/1¾ oz/50 g bittersweet/dark chocolate

2 tbsp/1 oz/25 g butter

½ cup/4 fl oz/125 ml heavy/double cream

1 tbsp sugar

1. Preheat the oven to 425°F/220°C/gas 7 and line a baking sheet with parchment paper.
2. On a lightly floured surface, roll the dough out to a rectangle measuring roughly 12 x 8 inches/30 x 20 cm. Cut the dough in half sideways. Brush one of the halves of dough with the melted butter, saving some for a final brush over before they go into the oven.
3. In a small bowl, mix together the sugar and cinnamon. Sprinkle three-quarters of the sugar mix over the buttered dough, then lay the unbuttered dough half on top. Using a rolling pin, gently roll to press the two halves together. Cut the dough into 10 even strips, roughly 1 inch/2.5 cm in thickness. Brush the tops of the strips with the remaining butter and sprinkle the remaining sugar on top.
4. Holding a strip at one end, twist it a few times to form a spiral and place onto the baking sheet. Repeat to make 10 sticks. Cook for about 10–12 minutes until golden.
5. While the sticks are cooking, make the chocolate sauce. Place all the ingredients in a small saucepan and gently warm over a low heat, stirring every so often, until you have a silky chocolate sauce.
6. Pour the chocolate sauce into a small bowl and serve with the sticks.

FREDDY FAZBEAR'S PIZZAPLEX
FREDDY FAZBEAR'S PIZZAPLEX

Bonnie's BURGERS & Subs

Sure, everyone in the Pizzaplex loves a slice and a breaded dip, but there's so much more for your taste buds to explore. Everyone's favorite rabbit animatronic, Bonnie, is on hand to kick things off with a fabulous master recipe for essential burgers. With meaty subs, skewers, salmon patties, fish bites, and more in this section, you won't be short of your din-spiration!

Bonnie's

BURGERLICIOUS BURGER MIX

Every awesome burger needs to begin with the basics. Get the meaty mix method and recipe right and the rest is a piece of cake. Well, a piece of burger, actually. Knowing how to rock out with a meaty treat is always cool around the Pizzaplex!

MAKES 4 BURGERS

PREPARATION TIME
10 MINUTES

COOKING TIME
10 MINUTES

WHAT YOU WILL NEED

- 1½ tbsp/⅔ oz/20 g butter
- 1 medium onion, very finely chopped
- 1lb 5 oz/600 g ground/minced beef chuck or brisket
- ½ tsp garlic powder
- ½ tsp onion powder
- ½ tsp black pepper
- 1 tsp salt
- 1 tbsp Worcestershire sauce
- 1 egg yolk

1. In a small pan over low heat, melt the butter and cook the finely chopped onion until soft. Make sure not to add any color to the onion. Remove from the heat and leave to cool completely.
2. In a large bowl, mix the meat and onions until well combined. Add the remaining ingredients and really mix well using your hands.
3. Divide into four even portions. If you have a burger press, great. If not, press the burger patties between two sheets of parchment paper, using the base of a saucepan to flatten them. Use right away, or chill in the fridge for a couple days or freeze until needed.

- ★ **This is the master recipe for the following four recipes. Once you make the mix, you don't need to make four burgers—you can adapt the mix for the following recipes and freeze any that you don't need immediately.**
- ★ **Shaping the burger mix into patties is a good way to store and freeze them, but if you know you're using the mix for the meatballs, just turn to the meatball recipe of your choice after you've portioned them out because you'll be adding more ingredients to the mix.**

Rabbits are cute
and cuddly, yeah?
Not so with
Bonnie—watch his
every move!

Bonnie's ULTIMATE BURGER

with crispy buttermilk onions

As a lead guitarist, it should be no surprise to see Bonnie leading the way with instructions on making the ultimate burger. If you top it with the crispy coated onions, you'll be striking all the right chords once again!

MAKES 2 BURGERS

PREPARATION TIME
45 MINUTES

COOKING TIME
20 MINUTES

WHAT YOU WILL NEED

FOR THE BURGER

2 patties Bonnie's Burgerlicious Burger Mix (see page 28)

2 burger buns

2 slices of cheese

Lettuce of your choice

2 slices of tomato

Sliced pickles

FOR THE ONIONS

1 small onion, thinly sliced

3 tbsp buttermilk

⅚ cup/7 fl oz/200 ml vegetable oil

2 tbsp all-purpose/plain flour

1 tsp paprika

Salt and black pepper

FOR THE BURGER SAUCE

2 tbsp mayonnaise

1 tsp ketchup

1 gherkin, finely chopped

1 tsp yellow mustard

1 tbsp finely chopped chives (optional)

1. Place the sliced onions into a bowl with the buttermilk and leave them to soak until you are ready to fry.
2. For the burger sauce, combine the ingredients in a small bowl and set to one side.
3. To fry the onions, heat the vegetable oil in a small saucepan or frying pan over medium heat.
4. Place the flour into another bowl, add the paprika, and season with salt and black pepper.
5. To test that the oil is hot enough, dip 1 or 2 pieces of onion into the flour and place into the oil. The oil is hot enough if the onion gets crispy after about a minute.
6. Fry the onions in batches until golden and crisp. Drain on paper towels.
7. To cook the burgers, heat a frying pan or griddle to medium-high heat.
8. Place the open buns facedown in the pan and toast until lightly browned.
9. Brush the patties with vegetable oil and cook for about 3–4 minutes. Flip the patties and add the cheese. Continue cooking for 3–4 minutes.
10. Now you are ready to build the ultimate burger. Spread the bun with some burger sauce. Add lettuce, tomato, the cheeseburger, pickles (if using), a generous amount of crispy onions, more burger sauce, and finally the top bun. Sit back and enjoy.

SECURITY BREACH Meatball Sub

Security guard Vanessa keeps a close eye on the Pizzaplex. Away from her annoying gaze, fire up the pan and grill to create a mighty meatball sub to remember. Saucy and scrumptious—that's the dish by the way, not Vanessa!

MAKES 2

PREPARATION TIME
30 MINUTES

COOKING TIME
25 MINUTES

WHAT YOU WILL NEED

2 portions Bonnie's Burgerlicious Burger Mix (see page 28)

1 tsp dried basil

1 tbsp vegetable oil

2 sub rolls, sliced

1 buffalo mozzarella ball, drained

Handful of arugula/rocket

FOR THE TOMATO SAUCE

1 tbsp olive oil

2 scallions/spring onions, chopped

1 garlic clove, chopped

¾ cup/5½ fl oz/175 ml tomato puree

1 jarred roasted red bell pepper, chopped

¼ tsp hot pepper/chili flakes

Salt and black pepper

1. Place the burger portions into a bowl and mix in the dried basil. Divide the mixture into 12 even portions and roll into meatballs.
2. Place a frying pan over medium heat, add the vegetable oil, and fry the meatballs until nicely browned, then transfer to a plate.
3. In the same pan, make the sauce. Add the olive oil and fry the scallions and garlic for about a minute. Pour in the tomato puree, add the roasted pepper and hot pepper flakes, and season with salt and pepper. Once simmering, place the meatballs into the sauce and simmer for 10 minutes.
4. While the sauce is cooking, preheat the broiler/grill and toast the cut sides of the sub rolls.
5. Place the bottoms of the toasted rolls onto a baking tray and spoon the meatballs and sauce on top. Add the mozzarella cheese and put back under the hot broiler to melt the cheese. Once melted, add half the arugula to each roll, top with the sub lids, and serve.

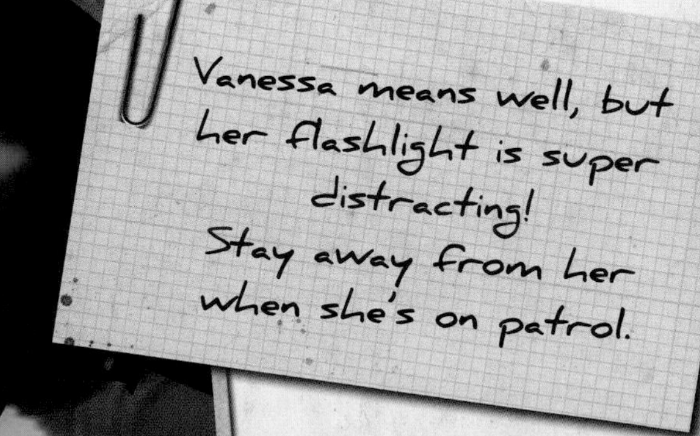

Lefty's MEAT BITE SKEWERS

Your patties take on a new shape as munch-tastic meat bite skewers. Lefty clearly likes the look of this quick but tasty dish, so join in and finish the plate before he laps it up!

SERVES 2

PREPARATION TIME
30 MINUTES

COOKING TIME
8 MINUTES

WHAT YOU WILL NEED

2 portions Bonnie's Burgerlicious Burger Mix (see page 28)

2 garlic cloves, crushed

1 tsp ground cumin

½ tsp ground coriander

½ tsp hot pepper/chili flakes

1 tbsp chopped flat leaf parsley

FOR THE COUSCOUS

¾ cup/5½ oz/150 g couscous

1 tsp harissa paste

1 cup/9 fl oz/250 ml boiling water

½ cup/3½ oz/100 g cucumber, peeled and chopped into small pieces

1 large tomato, seeded and chopped

Small handful of mint and cilantro/coriander leaves, chopped

TO SERVE

2 tbsp Greek yogurt

2 flatbreads

Lemon wedges

Sriracha sauce

You'll need 4 wooden or metal skewers for this!

1. Place the beef patties into a bowl. Add the garlic, cumin, coriander, hot pepper flakes, and parsley and mix well using your hands. Divide the mixture into four even portions.
2. Using slightly wet hands, roll each portion into a sausage shape, then thread a skewer through the middle, pressing the meat onto the skewer. Leave in the fridge for 20 minutes to firm up.
3. Put the couscous in a bowl. Place the harissa paste into a measuring cup, add the boiling water and stir. Pour the hot water over the couscous, cover with plastic wrap/cling film and leave to soak for 10–15 minutes.
4. While the couscous is soaking, preheat the broiler/grill to medium hot. Place the skewers onto a baking tray and cook for 7–8 minutes, turning regularly, until cooked through.
5. Fluff up the couscous with a fork and stir in the chopped cucumber, tomato, and herbs. Season with salt and black pepper.
6. Spoon the couscous onto a serving plate, top with the skewers, and serve with some Greek yogurt, warm flatbreads, lemon wedges, and some sriracha for a kick.

Lefty's real name is actually L.E.F.T.E. It stands for Lure Encapsulate Fuse Transport and Extract. Don't forget that now!

EL CHIP'S
Fully Loaded Tortillas

It's time to spice up a Mexican favorite. El Chip's is a vibrant restaurant found in the Pizzaplex, and this is the secret to its tasty tortillas. Starting with the pico de gallo, it's quick cuisine but with a kick you won't forget in a hurry!

SERVES 2

PREPARATION TIME
25 MINUTES

COOKING TIME
15 MINUTES

WHAT YOU WILL NEED

1 portion Bonnie's Burgerlicious Burger Mix (see page 28)
2 tbsp vegetable oil
1 small onion, finely chopped
2 garlic cloves, crushed
1 tbsp taco seasoning
1 cup /7 oz/200 g drained canned black beans
1 large bag of tortilla chips
1 cup/3½ oz/100 g grated cheddar cheese

FOR THE PICO DE GALLO

1 small red onion, finely chopped
1 jalapeño pepper, seeded and finely chopped
Juice of 1 lime
3 tomatoes, seeded and flesh finely chopped
1 tbsp chopped cilantro/coriander
Salt and black pepper

FOR TOPPING

1 avocado, chopped
½ cup/ 1¾ oz/50 g pickled jalapeños
2 scallions/spring onions, chopped
2 tbsp sour cream
Hot sauce (optional)
Cilantro/coriander leaves

1. To make the pico de gallo, mix the first five ingredients together and season with salt and pepper. Put in the fridge until needed.
2. Break up the burger patty with a fork. Add the oil to a frying pan and cook the onion and garlic for a couple minutes over medium heat. Add the broken patty and continue breaking it up as it cooks—you want it to be like ground beef, but crispy.
3. Add the taco seasoning, black beans, and a tablespoon of water. Cook for another 2 minutes, then remove from the heat. Preheat your broiler/grill.
4. Place half the tortilla chips onto an oven-safe serving tray. Top with half the meat. Arrange the remaining tortilla chips over the meat, then add the last of the meat and sprinkle the cheese on top. Put the dish under a broiler to melt the cheese.
5. Top the loaded tortilla chips with chopped avocado and jalapeños. Drizzle the sour cream on top of the fully loaded tortilla chips. Serve with the pico de gallo on the side, some hot sauce, if you like, and extra cilantro.

Freddy Fact

As well as the El Chip's eatery, look out for the El Chip's tortilla-style tortilla chips that can be picked up at the prize counter. There's even a bold and spicy flavor!

SALMON PATTIES

Prepared by Bonnie

The Bonnie Bowl is a legendary location, but instead of dishing up ice cream and drinks as usual, it has salmon patties on the menu today. Rabbit animatronic Bonnie is behind this fun fish-based dish, so get prepping the patties!

MAKES 2 PATTIES

PREPARATION TIME
20 MINUTES, PLUS CHILING

WHAT YOU WILL NEED

1 lb 5 oz/600 g fresh salmon, skinned and pin boned

1 small red chili, finely chopped

A thumb-sized piece of ginger, finely grated

Finely grated zest of 1 lime

1 tbsp chopped cilantro/coriander

1 tbsp fish sauce

1½ cups/2½ oz/75 g fresh bread crumbs

1. Chop the salmon into chunks and place in a food processor. Pulse a few times so the salmon breaks down, but make sure you keep some texture—don't pulse it to mush!
2. Put the salmon into a bowl. Add all the chopped fresh ingredients and the fish sauce and mix well. Stir in the bread crumbs—this will bring the mixture together and help hold the shape while cooking.
3. Divide the mixture into four portions and shape them into patties. Pop in the fridge to firm up for 30 minutes before using as directed in the recipe you are following.

★ Before you fry the patties, gently coat them in a little flour—this will help crisp them beautifully.

★ These are truly easy to make and can be used as the base for the following four recipes.

Ballora's SALMON BURGER

Feeling like making some moves, just like delicious dancer Ballora? You probably don't, but you will definitely want to make these scrumptious salmon burgers! Complete with a mega mango salsa, and they are lip-licking good.

MAKES 2

PREPARATION TIME
30 MINUTES

COOKING TIME
30 MINUTES

WHAT YOU WILL NEED

2 burger buns of your choice

1 tbsp all-purpose/plain flour

2 Salmon Patties (see page 38)

2 tbsp vegetable oil

Crisp lettuce of your choice

FOR THE MANGO SALSA

½ ripe mango, peeled, stoned, and diced

¼ red bell pepper, seeded and finely chopped

2 scallions/spring onions, finely chopped

1 red chili, seeded and finely chopped

1 garlic clove, crushed

Finely grated zest and juice of 1 lime

Handful of cilantro/coriander leaves

FOR THE SRIRACHA MAYO

2 tbsp mayonnaise

1 tsp sriracha

1. Make the mango salsa in advance—the longer it sits, the better the flavor. Combine all the ingredients well and leave in the fridge until needed.
2. For the sriracha mayo, mix the two ingredients together and set that aside, too.
3. Place a frying pan over medium heat. Toast the insides of the burger buns, then leave to one side.
4. Place the flour onto a plate. Dip the Salmon Patties in the flour to coat them evenly. Add the vegetable oil to the pan and, once hot, cook the patties for about 4 minutes on each side until golden and crisp.
5. Spread the base of a bun with half the sriracha mayo. Add the lettuce, followed by a patty. Top with a generous amount of the mango salsa and add the lid of the bun. Repeat to make the second burger and enjoy.

Ballora may look sweet and humanlike, but there's still plenty to be afraid of with this animatronic!

at Freddy's

Stage Fright
SALMON PATTY SUB

When Freddy, Roxy, Chica, and Monty are on stage together, it could give unsuspecting bystanders quite a fright! Relax them with a wonderful salmon patty sub that's topped with a curious cucumber pickle.

SERVES 2

PREPARATION TIME
25 MINUTES

COOKING TIME
5 MINUTES

WHAT YOU WILL NEED

2 Salmon Patties (see page 38)
2 tbsp all-purpose/plain flour
2 tbsp vegetable oil
2 sub rolls, sliced
Handful of watercress

FOR THE ZINGY MAYO

2 tbsp mayonnaise
5 mint leaves, chopped
Finely grated zest of ½ lemon

FOR THE PICKLED CUCUMBER

¼ cucumber, thinly sliced or peeled into ribbons
4 radishes, thinly sliced
½ tsp sea salt
1 tsp sugar
1 tbsp white wine vinegar
¼ tsp mustard seeds
¼ tsp nigella seeds
½ tsp chopped dill

1. Make the pickled cucumber first because it needs time for the flavor to develop. Place the cucumber and radish into a colander, sprinkle with salt, and leave for 10 minutes. Squeeze out the excess water and place into a bowl. Add the remaining ingredients and leave to one side until you need it.
2. Make a quick flavorsome mayo by mixing the mayonnaise with the chopped mint and lemon zest. Set this aside, too.
3. Break each Salmon Patty into four pieces. Roll each piece into a ball and then press it so they look like mini patties. Roll them in the flour to coat. Heat the oil in a nonstick frying pan and fry the salmon patties for 4 minutes, turning over halfway through cooking, until crisp and golden.
4. While the patties cook, preheat the broiler/grill and toast the cut sides of the sub rolls. Spread each of the sub roll bases with a dollop of the mayo and arrange half the watercress over each. Add the mini salmon patties and finish with the pickled cucumber and extra mayo, if you have any left.

Freddy Fact

Pick up plenty of Pizzaplex memorabilia, featuring your favorite animatronics, at Glamrock Gifts. Well worth a visit!

Mr. Hippo's Crispy Fish Bites & Spicy Rice

Feeling hungry? Mr. Hippo is pleased to introduce you to the delights of crispy fish bites. Served with spicy rice for an extra kick, it's another clever use of your salmon patties that's ideal for lunch or dinner.

SERVES 2

PREPARATION TIME
40 MINUTES

COOKING TIME
25 MINUTES

WHAT YOU WILL NEED

2 tbsp all-purpose/plain flour
1 egg, beaten
3 tbsp panko bread crumbs
2 Salmon Patties (see page 38)
Vegetable oil, for frying

FOR THE SPICY RICE

¾ cup/5½ oz/150 g basmati rice
2 tbsp olive oil
1 onion, finely chopped
2 garlic cloves, crushed
½ tsp ground turmeric
¼ tsp hot pepper/chili flakes
½ tsp paprika
½ red bell pepper, chopped
1¼ cups/10 fl oz/300 ml vegetable stock, cold
Scant ½ cup/1¾ oz/50 g frozen peas

FOR THE DIPPING SAUCE

1 tbsp mayonnaise
1 tbsp sour cream
1 garlic clove, crushed
Finely grated zest of ½ lemon
½ tsp chopped dill

TO SERVE

Nice salad leaves such as pea shoots, arugula/rocket, or watercress
Lemon wedges

1. Rinse the rice in cold water for a few minutes, then leave in a bowl of cold water for an additional 15 minutes.
2. While the rice is soaking, add the olive oil to a medium-sized pan with a lid and gently cook the onion until it starts to soften. Add the garlic, turmeric, hot pepper flakes, paprika, and red pepper and continue cooking for a few more minutes. Drain the rice and stir it into the pan.
3. Pour in the vegetable stock and peas and bring to a simmer. Once simmering, place the lid on and continue cooking for exactly 2 minutes, then turn the heat off and leave the pan without touching the lid for 15 minutes (it's really important not to remove the lid).
4. While the rice is resting, put the flour in a shallow bowl, the beaten egg in another bowl, and the panko bread crumbs into a third bowl. Break each Salmon Patty into four pieces and roll each piece into a ball. Roll the balls in the flour to coat, shaking off any excess, then into the beaten egg—making sure they have a good coating—and finally into the bread crumbs.
5. Pour oil into a saucepan to a depth of about 2 inches/5 cm and set it over medium heat. Once hot, cook the salmon bites in the hot oil for about 4 minutes, turning them occasionally. You can also do this in a fryer heated to 350°F/180°C, if you have one. Drain on paper towels/kitchen roll.
6. For the dipping sauce, mix all the ingredients together.
7. Divide the rice between your plates, and top with the salmon bites. Serve the dip on the side with some crisp leaves and a wedge or two of lemon.

Zingy SALMON LEMONGRASS SKEWERS *Bonnie Style*

Bonnie is back to inspire another rock 'n' roll dish, with added zing! Salmon lemongrass skewers are packed with pep but are also not overpowering. With the gorgeous noodle salad, this combo is a complete winner.

SERVES 2

PREPARATION TIME
40 MINUTES

COOKING TIME
8 MINUTES

WHAT YOU WILL NEED

2 Salmon Patties (see page 38)

4 sticks of lemongrass

Olive oil, for brushing

FOR THE SALAD

¾ cup/3¼ oz/90 g rice noodles

¼ cup/1¾ oz/50 g sugar snap peas, halved lengthwise

1 tsp sesame oil

3 scallions/spring onions, shredded

Small handful of torn cilantro/coriander

Small handful of mint leaves

FOR THE DRESSING

1 tbsp sesame oil

1 tbsp rice wine vinegar

Juice of 1 lime

1 tsp grated fresh ginger

1 tsp honey

TO SERVE

Sliced red chili

Black sesame seeds

10 cashew nuts, toasted and roughly chopped

Lime wedges

1. Divide both Salmon Patties into two, so you have four pieces. With slightly wet hands, form one of the pieces into a sausage shape, then thread a stalk of lemongrass through it, gently pressing so the salmon sticks to the skewer. Repeat with the remaining salmon and lemongrass to create four skewers, then pop them in the fridge to chill for about 30 minutes.
2. For the salad, place the rice noodles and sugar snaps into a bowl and pour boiling water from a kettle over them. Leave for 5 minutes, then drain, toss with the sesame oil, and leave to cool completely.
3. For the dressing, mix all the ingredients together, then pour over the noodles and toss gently. At this stage, turn your broiler/grill on to medium.
4. Place the salmon skewers onto a baking tray, brush with a little olive oil, and cook for about 8 minutes, turning three or four times while cooking, until the fish is cooked through.
5. Toss the spring onions, cilantro, and mint through the noodles and arrange onto two plates. Serve the skewers to the side and finish with sliced chili, sesame seeds, cashew nuts, and fresh lime wedges.

LET'S
EAT!!!

Chica's Chicken Choices

Chica is always on the prowl. However, when she's not marching around the Pizzaplex and banging on doors, she takes some time to inspire a range of yummy chicken choices. Fantastic burgers, Thai-style salad, chicken coconut curry, and pop-tastic bites are on the way, so listen up and let Chica take charge!

Chica's CRISPY FRIED CHICKEN

Pick up your chicken pieces and start making a mouthwatering meal full of spice and flavor. French fries and coleslaw are an added treat, but the focus is fully on this chicken-licious creation!

SERVES 2

PREPARATION TIME
30 MINUTES, PLUS
AT LEAST 2 HOUR MARINADE

COOKING TIME
25–40 MINUTES

WHAT YOU WILL NEED

1¼ cups/10 fl oz/284 ml buttermilk
1 tsp salt
4 bone-in chicken thighs
4 chicken drumsticks
Vegetable oil, for frying

FOR THE SPICE MIX

1 tsp smoked paprika
1 tsp black pepper
1 tsp garlic powder
1 tsp celery powder
½ tsp cayenne pepper
1 tsp dried oregano
½ tsp dried thyme

FOR THE COATING

1 cup/3½ oz/100 g cornstarch/cornflour
2 tbsp/⅔ oz/20 g cornmeal
¾ cup/3½ oz/100 g all-purpose/plain flour
1 tsp paprika
½ tsp ground turmeric

TO SERVE

French fries
Coleslaw

1. In a small bowl, combine all the spice mix ingredients and set aside.
2. Put the buttermilk in a medium bowl and whisk in 2 teaspoons of the spice mix and the salt. Place the chicken thighs and drumsticks into the buttermilk, making sure they are all well coated. Leave the bowl in the fridge for 2–3 hours, or ideally overnight.
3. For the coating, place all the ingredients into a large mixing bowl along with the remaining spice mix and season with a little salt.
4. To fry the chicken, fill a deep-sided pan to a depth of about 4 inches/10 cm with vegetable oil and, using a kitchen thermometer, heat to 350°F/180°C. You can also do this in a deep fryer. Preheat the oven to 275°F/140°C/gas 1.
5. Drain the chicken from the buttermilk, shaking off any excess, and toss in the coating. Coat each piece again by dipping it back into the buttermilk, then back into the coating. Shake off any excess and place onto a plate.
6. Working in batches, fry the chicken for about 10–12 minutes, turning occasionally, until golden and cooked through. Drain on paper towels/kitchen roll, then keep the chicken warm on a tray in the oven while you cook the remaining batches.
7. Serve the chicken with french fries and coleslaw.

Freddy's Top Tips!

★ **To make sure your chicken is cooked through, make a small cut into the meat and check that the juices run clear.**

Chica Chicken
FREDDY FAZBEAR'S PIZZAPLEX

Funtime Chica's HARISSA CHICKEN WINGS

Let the fun time continue with another chicken favorite packed with taste. These pieces need time to marinate, so don't rush and you'll be very pleased with your rewards . . .

SERVES 2

PREPARATION TIME
25 MINUTES, PLUS AT LEAST 2 HOUR MARINADE

COOKING TIME
30 MINUTES

WHAT YOU WILL NEED

Scant 1 cup/8 fl oz/225 ml buttermilk
3 tbsp harissa paste
2 lb 4 oz/1 kg chicken wings, cut in half
½ cup/1¾ oz/50 g cornstarch/cornflour
6 tbsp/1¾ oz/50 g all-purpose/plain flour
1 tsp salt
1 tsp ground black pepper
cooking oil spray
3 tbsp Frank's hot sauce (or other store-bought hot sauce)
2 tbsp honey
Juice of 1 lime

FOR TAHINI DIPPING SAUCE

1 tbsp tahini
Juice of 1 lemon
2 garlic cloves, crushed

TO SERVE

2 scallions/spring onions, chopped
Small handful of cilantro/coriander

1. In a large bowl, whisk together the buttermilk and 1 tablespoon of the harissa paste. Stir the chicken wings into the buttermilk so they are well covered and leave in the fridge to marinate for a couple hours or overnight.
2. When you're ready to cook, preheat your oven to 400°F/200°C/gas 6 and line a baking tray with parchment paper.
3. Put the cornstarch, all-purpose flour, and the salt and pepper into another large bowl and mix together. Drain the wings from the buttermilk and toss into the flour mix. Lay each wing onto the lined tray, leaving a little space between them. Spray the wings with cooking oil and bake for about 25–30 minutes, turning halfway through.
4. While the wings are cooking, mix the remaining harissa paste with the hot sauce, honey, and lime juice to make a glaze.
5. Make the tahini dipping sauce by whisking the ingredients together with 3 tablespoons water—sauce should be runny.
6. Once the wings are cooked, toss them in the spicy glaze, then arrange onto a serving plate. Sprinkle with scallions and cilantro and serve alongside the tahini dip.

Chica-Licious THAI PATTIES

Check out (or should that be "chick" out?!) how to create the perfect burger patties—Chica style! With a Thai flavor that gives an exciting kick, these are the base for the following recipes in this scrumptious section. Enjoy!

MAKES 4 PATTIES

PREPARATION TIME
25 MINUTES

WHAT YOU WILL NEED

4 skinless and boneless chicken breasts (roughly 1lb 5 oz/600 g)

1 egg, beaten

2 garlic cloves, crushed

5 scallions/spring onions, finely chopped

Zest and juice of 1 lime

1 tbsp soy sauce

1 tsp fish sauce

1 tbsp red Thai curry paste

1 tbsp chopped cilantro/coriander

2 cups/3½ oz/100 g fresh bread crumbs

1. Roughly chop the chicken into chunks and place in a food processor with the egg. Pulse a few times to mince the chicken, keeping some texture—don't overprocess it so it becomes too smooth.
2. Place the chicken into a large mixing bowl and add the garlic, scallions, lime zest and juice, soy sauce, fish sauce, Thai curry paste, and cilantro and mix well so everything is incorporated. Add the bread crumbs and stir well.
3. With slightly wet hands, divide the mixture into four portions and shape them into patties. Place the patties on a plate, cover, and chill in the fridge for 30 minutes before using.

Chica's Ultimate THAI CHICKEN BURGER

Chica's Thai burger has just the right level of spice, meaning you can serve up a chicken classic that's a winner all the way. Follow the super slaw and sauce recipes and your burger will get the most awesome accompaniment!

MAKES 2

PREPARATION TIME
30 MINUTES

COOKING TIME
10 MINUTES

WHAT YOU WILL NEED

2 Chica-Licious Thai Patties (see page 54)

1 tbsp vegetable oil

2 burger buns

Small handful of arugula/rocket

FOR THE SLAW

¼ cup /1¾ oz/50 g red cabbage, finely shredded

1 carrot, peeled and sliced into matchsticks

½ red onion, finely sliced

½ red chili, seeded and finely chopped

Juice of a lime

½ tbsp honey

1 garlic clove, crushed

1 tbsp rice wine vinegar

½ tbsp soy sauce

Handful of cilantro/coriander, torn

FOR THE SAUCE

2 tbsp mayonnaise

2 tsp Thai sweet chili sauce

1. First task is to make the slaw. Mix all the ingredients together in a large bowl and leave for about 15 minutes to let the flavors mix.
2. Heat up a frying pan over medium heat. Toast the inside of the burger buns and leave to one side.
3. Add the vegetable oil to the pan and, once hot, cook the patties for 3–4 minutes on each side until browned and cooked through.
4. While the patties are cooking, mix the mayonnaise with the sweet chili sauce and spread onto the base of the buns.
5. Add a handful of the arugula to each bun, followed by a chicken patty and a generous amount of the slaw. Place the lids on and enjoy.

On the Prowl . . .

COCONUT CURRY

Chica can be a relentless animatronic, and that's reflected in this chicken coconut curry that can really pack a punch! Of course, the coconut milk is a silky-smooth ingredient and you can dial down on the Thai paste and chili for a lighter flavor.

SERVES 2

PREPARATION TIME
30 MINUTES

COOKING TIME
20 MINUTES

WHAT YOU WILL NEED

2 Chica-Licious Thai Patties (see page 54)

2 tbsp vegetable oil

⅔ cup/5½ fl oz/150 ml chicken stock

1 (14 oz/400 g) can coconut milk

2 tbsp green or red Thai curry paste

½ cup/1¾ oz/50 g green beans, cut in half

⅓ cup/1¾ oz/50 g bamboo shoots

A thumb-sized piece of ginger, grated

3 scallions/spring onions, cut into 1¼ inches/3 cm pieces

Juice of 1 lime

Large green chili, seeded and sliced

TO SERVE

Steamed white rice

Thai basil or cilantro/coriander

1. Divide each of the patties into five pieces and roll them into balls. Heat a nonstick frying pan over medium heat, add the vegetable oil, and cook the meatballs until seared, then remove them from the pan.
2. Using the same pan, pour in the chicken stock, coconut milk, and curry paste and bring to a simmer, stirring as you go. Add the green beans, bamboo shoots, ginger, and scallions, and return the meatballs to the pan, too. Simmer for 5 minutes, making sure the chicken balls are cooked through.
3. Just before you are ready to serve, squeeze in the lime juice, add the green chili, and season to taste. Serve with some steamed rice and Thai basil or cilantro, if you have it.

Chica's Fiery THAI CHICKEN SALAD!!!

Even with bite-sized chicken pieces, this Thai chicken salad is still a big deal and is great for lunch or dinner! The dressing and salad is a mouthwatering mixture, forming a succulent bed to sprinkle your pieces over. Crank up the chilies if you dare!

MAKES 2 SALADS

PREPARATION TIME
45 MINUTES

COOKING TIME
20 MINUTES

WHAT YOU WILL NEED

2 Chica-Licious Thai Patties (see page 54)
1 tbsp vegetable oil
½ pointed cabbage, shredded
2 carrots, peeled and coarsely grated
2 scallions/spring onions, finely sliced
½ cup/2½ oz/75 g bean sprouts
⅓ cup/1¾ oz/50 g radishes, thinly sliced
¼ cucumber, halved, seeds scraped out and thinly sliced
1 tbsp mint leaves, torn
1 tbsp cilantro/coriander, torn
Thai basil (optional)
Crispy onions (for garnish)
Thai crackers (for garnish)

FOR THE DRESSING
2 tbsp rice wine vinegar
1 tbsp soy sauce
1 tsp sugar
Juice of 1 lime
2 tbsp fish sauce
1–2 bird's eye chilies, deseeded and finely chopped
1 tbsp peanut butter

1. In a large bowl, mix together all the salad vegetables and herbs.
2. In a separate bowl, whisk together the rice vinegar, soy, sugar, lime juice, fish sauce, and peanut butter to make a smooth dressing. Mix in the chilies to add spice.
3. In a frying pan over medium heat, add the vegetable oil. When hot, cook the chicken patties for 3–4 minutes on each side until crisp, golden, and cooked through. Remove pan from heat and allow the patties to cool slightly.
4. Slice the chicken patties into bite-sized pieces.
5. Pour half the dressing into the salad and mix to coat. Divide into serving bowls, top with the sliced chicken and a few crispy onions. Serve with the Thai crackers, and put the remaining dressing in a cup on the side.

Nedd Bear's POPPING CHICKEN BITES

Have you noticed the lovely whiff of popcorn around the Pizzaplex? There's no escaping it, so embrace it and try this chicken twist using the classic snack. Apparently, the idea "popped" into Nedd Bear's animatronic head. Good work, Nedd!

MAKES 20

PREPARATION TIME
35 MINUTES

COOKING TIME
15 MINUTES

WHAT YOU WILL NEED

½ cup/1¾ oz/50 g panko bread crumbs

2 tbsp plain popcorn

½ cup/1 oz/30 g all-purpose/plain flour

1 tsp garlic powder

3 tbsp buttermilk

2 Chica-Licious Thai Patties (see page 54)

Vegetable oil, for frying

FOR THE CHILI DIPPING SAUCE

1 tbsp hot pepper flakes/chili flakes

2½ oz/75 g granulated sugar

3½ tbsp/1¾ fl oz/50 ml rice wine vinegar

2 garlic cloves, finely grated

2 tsp cornstarch/corn flour

Pinch of salt

TO SERVE

Scallions/spring onions

Sliced red chili

Cilantro/coriander

1. Start by making the chili sauce. Put the hot pepper flakes, sugar, vinegar, garlic, and scant ½ cup/3½ fl oz/100 ml water into a small saucepan. Simmer over low heat until the sugar has dissolved. Mix the cornstarch with a tablespoon of water to form a paste. Pour into the chili sauce and stir—it should thicken within a few seconds. Season with salt, then take the sauce off the heat and leave to cool.
2. Put the bread crumbs and popcorn into a food processor and pulse until you have a course crumb. Put into a bowl.
3. In a second bowl, mix the flour and garlic powder. Put the buttermilk in a third bowl.
4. Break the chicken patties into bite-size pieces—you should get roughly 10 from each patty. Roll them into little balls, then toss them in the flour. Dip them into the buttermilk, letting the excess drip off, before finally tossing them into the popcorn crumb.
5. Pour oil to a depth of 1 inch/2.5 cm in a deep-sided pan and heat it to about 350°F/180°C. If you put a cube of bread in the oil, it should turn golden in about 1 minute—or you can use a kitchen thermometer. Working in small batches, cook the chicken for about 3–4 minutes until golden and cooked through, then drain on paper towels/kitchen roll.
6. Place all the cooked popcorn chicken on a serving plate and garnish with spring onions, some shredded chilies and cilantro leaves. Add the chili sauce to a small bowl and serve on the side.

Foxy's PORK Plates

Pirate animatronic Foxy is as cunning as they come! Mercifully, the following selection of perfect pork plates are anything but shifty and sly. Get ready to pull out some great meaty treats, from pulled pork to sloppy burgers, tacos, and quesadillas. Yummy for your tummy!

Foxy's PULLED PORK

Master Recipe

Dashing around the Pizzaplex can be a race against time. Relax, though, as this pulled pork master recipe needs plenty of time in the oven. It's quick to prep and is a delicious dish dripping with succulent flavor!

SERVES 3-4

PREPARATION TIME
15 MINUTES

COOKING TIME
5 HOURS

WHAT YOU WILL NEED

- 1 tbsp ground cumin
- 1 tsp black pepper
- 1 tsp smoked paprika
- 1 tbsp brown sugar
- 1 tsp salt
- 4½ lb/2 kg boneless pork shoulder
- 1¼ cups/10 fl oz/300 ml cider
- Scant 1 cup/9 fl oz/250 ml Foxy's Quick 'n' Easy BBQ Sauce (see page 68)

1. Preheat the oven to 275°F/140°C/gas mark 1.
2. In a bowl, mix together all the spices, sugar, and salt. Rub the mixture all over the pork until completely covered. Place the pork in a casserole dish, pour in the cider, cover with a lid or foil, and cook for about 5 hours until the pork falls apart. Check the pork occasionally.
3. Once the pork is ready and falling apart, gently lift it from the casserole dish and place on a tray. Skim any excess fat from the juices left in the dish, then add about a cup/9 fl oz/250 ml of the BBQ sauce to the juices and mix.
4. Shred the pork with a couple forks, making sure to remove any fatty bits. Pop all the shredded pork back into the dish and mix into the BBQ sauce. This keeps the pork succulent. You can keep the pulled pork in the fridge for 3–4 days or freeze some to use later.

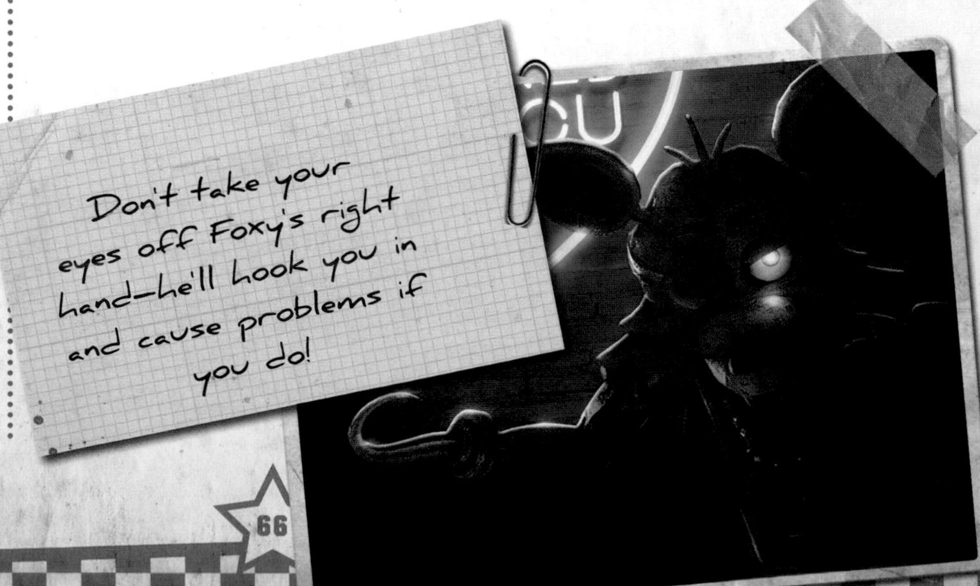

Foxy's Quick 'n' Easy BBQ SAUCE

In the Pizzaplex, there's no need to open a kitchen cupboard door for a bottle of BBQ sauce. Make your own sweet and smoky special sauce in just a few minutes with this super-slick guide!

MAKES 1 CUP

PREPARATION TIME
5 MINUTES

COOKING TIME
10 MINUTES

WHAT YOU WILL NEED

1 cup/9 oz/250 g tomato ketchup

3½ tbsp/1¾ fl oz/50 ml white wine vinegar

3¼ tbsp/1½ oz/40 g dark brown sugar

1 tbsp Worcestershire sauce

½ tsp mustard powder

1 tsp smoked paprika

Milled black pepper

1. Put all the ingredients into a medium saucepan and bring to a steady simmer over low heat. Once the sugar has dissolved, turn the heat up a little and boil for 2–3 minutes, then remove from the heat and leave to cool. This sauce will keep for a few weeks in the fridge.

Foxy's eye patch doesn't seem to hinder him as he's always on the lookout for intruders!

Freddy Fact

While you don't have to open kitchen doors for BBQ sauce, a Freddy Photo Pass literally does open doors for you around the Pizzaplex!

Foxy's Sloppy PULLED PORK BURGER

This pulled pork in a burger bun is such a glorious combo. The secret here is the quick pickle sauce that's spread over the succulent pork. Grab your ingredients and get busy creating a mouthwatering meal in no time!

SERVES 2

PREPARATION TIME
20 MINUTES

COOKING TIME
12–15 MINUTES

WHAT YOU WILL NEED

1 cup/9 oz/200 g Foxy's Pulled Pork (see page 66)

Scant ½ cup/3½ fl oz/100 ml Foxy's Quick 'n' Easy BBQ Sauce (see page 68)

2 burger buns

4 cheese slices

1 fresh jalapeño, sliced

FOR THE PICKLE

25 ml white wine vinegar

25 g sugar

1 star anise

1 tsp mustard seeds

¼ cucumber, thinly sliced

5 radishes, thinly sliced

1. To make the pickle, put the white wine vinegar, sugar, star anise, mustard seeds, and 3½ tablespoons water into a small saucepan. Simmer over medium-low heat until the sugar has dissolved.
2. While the liquid is warming, place the sliced cucumber and radishes in a small bowl. Pour the hot pickle liquid over the cucumbers and radishes, toss, and leave to the side while you get everything else ready. Don't forget to remove the star anise!
3. Put the pulled pork in a saucepan with plenty of BBQ sauce and place over low heat to warm through.
4. Toast the inside of the burger buns under a hot broiler/grill. Place a slice of cheese over the base of each burger bun and place back under the broiler to melt the cheese.
5. Top the cheese with the pulled pork, dividing it evenly between the buns. Add a generous amount of pickles and finish with the sliced jalapeño. Place the lids on and enjoy.

LOCAL NEWS

Local pizzeria said to close by year's end.

After a long struggle to stay in business after the tragedy that took place there many years ago, Freddy Fazbear's Pizza has announced that it will close by year's end.

Despite a year-long search for a buyer, companies seem unwilling to be associated with the company.

"These characters will live on. In the hearts of kids- these characters will live on." - CEO

SHAKES

Pulled Pork Tacos

It's a total games fest inside the Fazer Blast laser tag arena. When there's a break in the action, tuck into some special pulled pork tacos that come with a pickled onion that's packed with flavor. This recipe always hits the target!

SERVES 2

PREPARATION TIME
25 MINUTES

COOKING TIME
10 MINUTES

WHAT YOU WILL NEED

1 cup/9 oz/200 g Foxy's Pulled Pork (see page 66)

4 soft taco wraps

1 head Bibb lettuce/butter lettuce, shredded

1½ oz/40 g red cabbage, shredded

1 small avocado, cut into chunks

Sour cream, to drizzle

Sriracha sauce, to drizzle

FOR THE PICKLED ONION

1 red onion, thinly sliced into rings

2 tbsp/1fl oz/25 ml white wine vinegar

3 tbsp/1 oz/25 g sugar

1. To make the pickled onion, warm the white wine vinegar, sugar, and 2 tbsp/1 fl oz/25 ml water in a small pan. Once hot, remove from the heat, add the red onion, mix, and leave to cool.
2. Warm up the pulled pork in a saucepan or in the microwave. Heat the tacos in a dry frying pan.
3. To assemble, place a taco onto a plate, add some shredded lettuce and red cabbage, then a quarter of the pulled pork, followed by some avocado chunks and pickled red onion. Finish with a drizzle each of sour cream and sriracha.

Freddy Fact

Calling all recruits! Fazer Blast is a high-intensity space combat simulation! Suit up and save the universe as you blast everyone and everything with high-tech laser effects! Blast strangers, blast your friends! Beat the Superstar Score and get a free Fazer Blaster gun. Enlist now!

SNACK SPACE
DEFEAT YOUR HUNGER
Don't forget your Party
Pass for entry to Fazer
Blast! And make sure you
use the Fazerblaster to
stun attacking animatronics.
Blaster Return

Funtime Freddy's Dirty Wedges

With Pulled Pork & Pickled Salsa

Another pork masterpiece to entertain the crowds! Load up plates with flavorsome wedges, topped with lip-licking pulled pork and melted cheese. Such a showstopper!

SERVES 2

PREPARATION TIME
20 MINUTES

COOKING TIME
12–15 MINUTES

WHAT YOU WILL NEED

- 1 ½ lb/700 g potatoes
- 2 tbsp olive oil
- 1 tsp ground cumin
- 1 tsp ground coriander
- ½ tsp smoked paprika
- 1 tsp black pepper
- 1 tsp sea salt
- 5 sprigs of rosemary, roughly chopped

FOR THE TOPPING

- 1 cup/9 oz/200 g Foxy's Pulled Pork (see page 66)
- 1½ cups/5½ oz/150 g grated cheddar cheese
- 2–3 tbsp sour cream

FOR THE SALSA

- 3 scallions/spring onions, finely chopped
- 5 pickles, finely chopped
- 1 jalapeño, finely chopped
- 1 tbsp roughly chopped cilantro/coriander
- 1 beefsteak tomato, seeded and diced

1. Preheat the oven to 400°F/200°C/gas 6. Chop the potatoes into wedges, making sure they are roughly similar sizes so they cook evenly. Place the potatoes in a pan of water, bring to a boil, then cook for 5 minutes. Drain the potatoes into a colander, then leave them to cool in their own steam.
2. Place the potatoes into a roasting pan and drizzle over the olive oil. In a bowl, mix together the spices, salt, and rosemary, then sprinkle it over the potatoes and toss so the wedges are evenly coated. Roast for about 30–40 minutes until crisp.
3. For the salsa, put the chopped scallions, pickles, jalapeño, cilantro, and tomato into a bowl and mix together.
4. A few minutes before the wedges are ready, warm the pulled pork in a saucepan and turn on the broiler/grill. Place the wedges onto an ovenproof serving tray, top with the cheese, and place under the broiler until the cheese melts.
5. Top the wedges with the pulled pork and serve with a side of the salsa and some sour cream.

FAZCADE

Pulled Pork Quesadillas

Looking for something to entertain you? The Fazcade is full of exciting arcade machines, but how about taking on a Mexican quesadilla dish instead? This recipe has layers of lovely ingredients and makes great use of your prepared pulled pork.

SERVES 2

PREPARATION TIME
25 MINUTES

COOKING TIME
15 MINUTES

WHAT YOU WILL NEED

4 large flour tortillas

¼ cup/2 oz/60 g refried beans

Scant 1 cup/3 oz/80 g grated cheddar cheese

½ cup/4½ oz/120 g Foxy's Pulled Pork (see page 66)

⅓ cup/1¾ oz/50 g corn

½ red bell pepper chopped

Pickled jalapeño, finely sliced

10 g cilantro/coriander

TO SERVE

Lettuce leaves

Sour cream

Chili Dipping Sauce (see page 62, optional)

1. Heat a large nonstick pan on medium heat—make sure the pan is big enough to fit a tortilla. Spread the refried beans over two of the tortillas. Top both tortillas with a quarter of the cheese, the pulled pork, corn, red pepper, jalapeño, and cilantro. Sprinkle the remaining cheese over the top and sandwich the ingredients in by topping this with the other tortillas. Press down gently to compact the ingredients and seal the tortillas.

2. Carefully pick up one of the quesadillas and place it into the preheated pan. Cook until golden and crisp on the bottom, then carefully turn the quesadilla over and toast the other side. Place the quesadilla onto a board and slice into wedges while you cook the remaining one.

3. Serve the quesadillas on a board with crisp lettuce, sour cream, and a spicy chili dip, if you are using.

Freddy Fact

The Fazcade is also known as the West Arcade to some Freddy fans. It has three floors and plenty to keep visitors busy!

When investigating the
Fazcade ballroom, be
careful not to wake the
DJ Music Man.
He is not a nice fellow!

Glamrock Freddy's

FAVES & CLASSIC DISHES

As if to prove the animatronics can be creatures of habit, they never turn their noses away from a favorite dish. The Pizzaplex is home to a selection of classic cuisine. Featuring flavorsome fajitas, mac 'n' cheese, and gorgeous hot dogs, there's much to be said for a good old-fashioned fave!

Glamrock Freddy's MAC 'N' CHEESE

Surely no visitors to the Pizzaplex can resist a lovely helping of traditional mac 'n' cheese? It takes a little prep time in the kitchen, but the wait is always worth it when the bubbling dish comes out of the oven. Simply leave out the chorizo for your "not meat" option.

SERVES 6

PREPARATION TIME
30 MINUTES

COOKING TIME
40 MINUTES

WHAT YOU WILL NEED

1 ½ cups/7 oz/200 g elbow macaroni pasta

2 tbsp olive oil

1 onion, finely chopped

2 garlic cloves, crushed

¾ cup/4½ oz/125 g chorizo, roughly chopped

3½ tbsp/1 oz/30 g all-purpose/plain flour

3½ cups/28 fl oz/800 ml whole milk

3½ cups/10½ oz/300 g grated cheddar cheese

Scant 1 cup/2 oz/60 g grated Parmesan cheese

8 sundried tomatoes, chopped

¾ cup/3½ oz/100 g frozen peas

¾ cup/3½ oz/100 g kale, roughly chopped

⅓ cup/2½ oz/75 g fresh bread crumbs

Sea salt and milled black pepper

1. Cook the pasta in a large pot of boiling water for 5–6 minutes, then drain into a colander and leave to one side. Preheat your oven to 350°F/180°C/gas mark 4.
2. Heat the olive oil in a large saucepan, add the onion, and cook over a low heat until soft. Try not to color the onion. Add the garlic and chorizo to the pan and continue cooking for 5 minutes.
3. Stir in the flour and, once incorporated, start adding the milk a little at a time. Keep stirring and adding the milk until you have a smooth sauce. Stir in 3 cups/9 oz/250 g of the cheddar cheese and ⅔ cup/1½ oz/40 g of the Parmesan cheese and mix well. Season with a little salt and milled pepper.
4. Add the chopped sundried tomatoes, peas, and kale. Add the pasta and mix. Pour the mixture into a baking dish and spread so that it is even.
5. In a bowl, combine the bread crumbs and the remaining cheddar and Parmesan cheeses. Sprinkle the bread crumb mixture over the pasta and bake for about 30 minutes until golden and bubbling.

Freddy Fact

To get the full glitz and glory, visit the Famous GlamRock Beauty Salon. It's easy to find, right next to Roxy Raceway!

Glamrock Freddy's
FULLY LOADED HOT DOGS

Ready to relish another meaty treat? Well, the gherkin relish served with Glamrock Freddy's fully loaded dogs is a must-have extra alongside the crispy onions, crispy bacon, and drizzled mustard and ketchup. It could almost make an animatronic drool!

SERVES 4

PREPARATION TIME
20 MINUTES

COOKING TIME
10 MINUTES

WHAT YOU WILL NEED

2 slices bacon

4 large hot dogs

4 hot dog buns

4 tbsp sauerkraut

4 tbsp crispy onions

American mustard

Ketchup

FOR THE GHERKIN RELISH

2–3 medium gherkins, finely chopped

5 pickled jalapeños, finely chopped

½ small red onion, finely chopped

1 tsp honey

1 tsp whole-grain or Dijon mustard

½ tsp chopped dill

1. To make the relish, mix all the prepared ingredients in a bowl.
2. Heat a griddle pan over high heat. Add the bacon slices and cook for a few minutes until crisp. Remove the bacon slices from the griddle and allow to cool, then chop them into small pieces.
3. Turn the heat under the griddle down to medium and place the hot dogs on it. Heat the hot dogs through, turning them occasionally.
4. Open the buns and fill each with a tablespoon of the sauerkraut, then top each with a hot dog. Spoon some gherkin relish, crispy bacon bits, and crispy onions over the hot dogs and drizzle with mustard and ketchup.

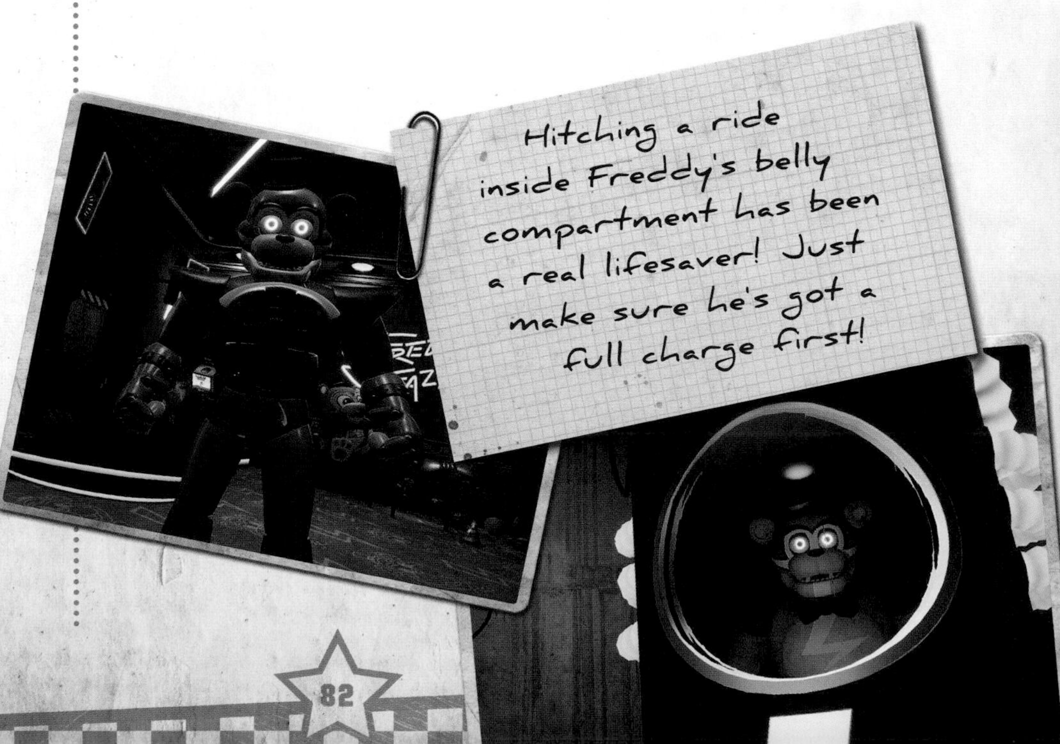

Balloon Boy's CHICKEN & CHORIZO FAJITAS

Balloon Boy is not "kidding" around when he says these classic fajitas will keep the whole family happy! They are easy to make and will load you up for your next animatronic encounter.

SERVES 2

PREPARATION TIME
20 MINUTES

COOKING TIME
12–15 MINUTES

WHAT YOU WILL NEED

4 tbsp olive oil

1 large chicken breast, thinly sliced

¼ cup/1¾ oz/50 g chorizo sausage, roughly chopped

1 small red onion, sliced

½ yellow bell pepper, seeded and cut into strips

2 tsp fajita seasoning

1 tbsp chopped cilantro/coriander

TO SERVE

4 flour tortillas

Lime wedges, for squeezing

Pickled jalapeños, chopped

Arugula/rocket

Small handful cilantro/coriander

Sour cream

1. Heat a large frying pan or wok over medium-high heat. Add 2 tbsp of olive oil to the pan and fry the chicken slices until seared all over and starting to brown. Remove the chicken from the pan and put onto a plate.
2. Now add the remaining olive oil and fry the chorizo, onion, and pepper for 3–4 minutes until they start to soften. Add the chicken back to the pan along with the fajita seasoning and toss everything together. Cook for another minute, then stir in the chopped cilantro and spoon into a serving bowl.
3. Heat the tortillas in a dry pan until you have a little color on them.
4. Serve the chicken filling with the tortillas, squeeze a little lime juice on them, and top with some jalapeños, arugula, cilantro, and a dollop of sour cream. Enjoy.

Bonnie's Buddha BOWL

The Bonnie Bowl is certainly an intriguing place, but forget about that and take on the Bonnie-inspired Buddha Bowl instead. This popular offering is a traditional vegetarian dish, loaded with several foods and served cold. Enjoy!

MAKES 2

PREPARATION TIME
40 MINUTES

COOKING TIME
20 MINUTES

WHAT YOU WILL NEED

3½ oz/100 g firm tofu, cut into bite-size chunks

2 tbsp olive oil

1 tbsp maple syrup

1 tbsp soy sauce

¾ cup/3½ oz/100 g drained canned chickpeas

1 tsp dry harissa spice mix

1 small red onion, thinly sliced

1 tbsp rice wine vinegar

1 tsp sugar

2 cups/9 oz/250 g cooked brown rice

1 medium zucchini/courgette, spiralized (or sliced, if you prefer)

⅔ cup/2 oz/60 g cooked broccoli

5 radishes, sliced

⅔ cup/2 handfuls of baby spinach

⅓ cup/3½ oz/100 g cooked lentils

2 tbsp hummus

Sesame, nigella, and pumpkin seeds, to sprinkle

Sriracha sauce, to drizzle

Sea salt

1. In a frying pan over medium heat, fry the tofu in 1 tbsp of olive oil until it starts to crisp. Add the maple syrup and soy sauce and continue cooking until glazed, turning frequently and starting to turn sticky. Remove from the pan and leave to cool.
2. Wash the pan and place back on the heat. Add the last of the olive oil and fry the chickpeas over high heat until they start to blister and char. Remove from the heat, add the harissa to the pan, toss the chickpeas to coat them, and leave to cool.
3. Place the red onion into a small bowl and toss with the rice wine vinegar and sugar. Leave to the side.
4. When assembling a Buddha bowl, it's important to keep all the ingredients separate in their own little piles. Divide the rice between the two bowls. Sprinkle the zucchini with a little salt and place onto the rice, dividing it evenly between the bowls. Add the broccoli, radishes, baby spinach, tofu pieces, chickpeas, lentils, and pickled red onions on top.
5. Add a spoonful of hummus to the center of each bowl. Sprinkle some pumpkin, nigella, and sesame seeds on top, then finish with a generous drizzle of the sriracha sauce.

Glamrock Chica's Breakfast Best

While the Pizzaplex is well known for its pizzas, burgers, and other marvelous meals, you may think breakfast doesn't feature much on the menu. Not so, and this section serves up a few early-morning recipes to get your day off to a great start. After spending the night in this place, that's got to be a good thing!

EGGS BENEDICT

with Glamrock Glamour

If you prefer your muffins a little more hot-blooded, go down the Glamrock route for extra entertainment. These eggs Benedict come with the meaty kick of chorizo sausage and chipotle paste to make breakfast go with a bang!

SERVES 2

PREPARATION TIME
30 MINUTES

COOKING TIME
20 MINUTES

WHAT YOU WILL NEED

2 tbsp white wine vinegar

1 tbsp olive oil

⅔ cup/3½ oz/100 g chorizo, chopped

10 cherry tomatoes, halved

4 eggs

2 English muffins

FOR THE AVOCADO SALSA

1 ripe avocado

1 tbsp red onion, finely chopped

1 tsp chopped cilantro/coriander, plus extra to serve

Squeeze of lime juice

Salt and black pepper

FOR THE HOLLANDAISE

½ cup/4½ oz/125 g butter

2 egg yolks

2 tsp white wine vinegar

A squeeze of lime juice and a little zest

½ tsp chipotle paste

1. Fill a large saucepan, big enough to hold 4 eggs, about 2–2½ inches/5–6 cm deep with water. Add the white wine vinegar and bring to a steady simmer. Reduce to the lowest heat.
2. While the water is heating, make the spicy hollandaise sauce. Melt the butter in the microwave. Put the egg yolks, vinegar, and lime juice and zest in a blender and mix for about 10 seconds. While still blending, slowly pour the melted butter into the egg mixture, making sure the whey (the white stuff at the bottom of the bowl) doesn't go in. When all the clear butter has been used, add the chipotle paste, blend for 2 seconds to mix, then pour the sauce into a serving bowl.
3. Heat the olive oil in a frying pan and add the chorizo and tomatoes. Cook over medium heat until the chorizo has crisped. Leave to one side.
4. For the avocado salsa, scoop the avocado flesh into a bowl. Add the red onion, cilantro, and a squeeze of lime juice, and season with salt and pepper.
5. Carefully crack the eggs into the hot water and leave to cook for about 3 minutes. You want a runny yolk but the whites to set.
6. Cut the muffins in half, then toast them and place onto serving plates. Divide the avocado salsa between the muffins, followed by the chorizo and tomato mixture. Lift the eggs out of the water with a slotted spoon and drain briefly. Place the eggs onto the muffins, pour the hollandaise sauce over the eggs, and serve with a little extra cilantro.

Five
at

The Puppet's
V-EGG-IE BENEDICT

A little care is required in creating this beauty of a breakfast dish, but patience and precision are rewarded with a lovely morning munchie that has a veggie blast. The Puppet is pulling all the right strings again!

SERVES 2

PREPARATION TIME
30 MINUTES

COOKING TIME
20 MINUTES

WHAT YOU WILL NEED

2 tbsp white wine vinegar

1½ tbsp/⅔ oz/20 g butter

¾ cup/3½ oz/100 g mushrooms, roughly sliced or chopped

1 ¼ cups/2¾ oz/80 g kale/cavolo nero

4 eggs

2 English muffins

FOR THE HOLLANDAISE SAUCE

½ cup/4¼ oz/120 g butter

2 egg yolks

1 tsp white wine vinegar

Squeeze of lemon juice

1 tsp chopped chives, dill, or parsley

Salt and black pepper

1. Fill a large saucepan, big enough to hold 4 eggs, about 2–2½ inches/5–6 cm deep with water. Add the white wine vinegar and bring to a steady simmer. Reduce to the lowest heat.
2. While the water is heating, make the hollandaise sauce. Melt the butter in a bowl in the microwave. Put the egg yolks, vinegar, and a squeeze of lemon juice in a blender and season with a little salt and pepper. Mix for about 10 seconds, then, while still blending, slowly pour the melted butter into the egg mixture, making sure the whey (the white stuff at the bottom of the bowl) doesn't go in. When all the clear butter has been used, add the herbs, blend for 2 seconds to mix, then pour the sauce into a serving bowl.
3. In a separate pan, melt the 1½ tbsp/⅔ oz/20 g of butter and add the mushrooms and kale. Cook until wilted and the mushrooms start to color, then season with salt and pepper.
4. Carefully crack the eggs into the hot water and leave to cook for about 3 minutes. You want a runny yolk but the whites to set.
5. Cut the muffins in half, then toast them and place onto serving plates. Divide the mushroom and kale mix between the muffins. Lift the eggs out of the water with a slotted spoon and drain briefly. Place the eggs onto the muffins. Pour the hollandaise sauce over the eggs and serve.

Moondrop's BLUEBERRY PANCAKES

Moondrop Sleepy-Time Candy is described as a relaxing snack just before bedtime. These new Moondrop blueberry pancakes are so luscious you'll struggle to sleep at night while dreaming about their yumminess.

SERVES 4

PREPARATION TIME
20 MINUTES

COOKING TIME
20 MINUTES

WHAT YOU WILL NEED

2 tsp/⅓ oz/10 g butter

1 cup/5½ oz/150 g blueberries

1½ cups/7 oz/200 g self-rising flour

1 tsp baking powder

Pinch of salt

1 large egg

1 cup/9 fl oz/250 ml whole milk

Vegetable oil, for frying

Maple syrup, to serve

1. Melt the butter in a small pan, then add ⅔ cup/3½ oz/100 g of the blueberries and cook until slightly soft. Leave to cool.
2. In a large bowl combine the flour, baking powder, and salt. Make a well in the center and crack in the egg. Pour in the milk and whisk until you have a smooth batter, then fold in the cooled blueberries.
3. Heat 1 teaspoon of vegetable oil in a large nonstick frying pan over medium heat. Drop large spoonfuls of the batter into the pan, spacing them out—you should be able to cook three pancakes per batch. Cook them until small bubbles appear on the surface, then flip the pancakes over and cook for another 30 seconds or until golden and cooked through. Keep the pancakes warm while you repeat the process to cook the rest of the batter.
4. Serve the pancakes with the remaining blueberries and maple syrup.

Don't be duped by the sleepy-looking images of Moondrop, because he's a nightmare animatronic during the dark!

Freddy Fact

Do you know what the opposite of Moondrop Sleepy-Time Candy is? Sunnydrop Energizing Candy of course!

Roxanne Wolf's Sweet Things

With the trials and tribulations of a trip to the Pizzaplex, it's common to begin yearning for home sweet home. Pay attention to the following delicious desserts and your home really will become a place of tasty after-dinner treats. Roxanne Wolf is always on the hunt for a sweet treat!

Roxanne Wolf's CHOCOLATE & CHERRY MOUSSE

Bring a touch of rock star glamour with this high-octane chocolate and cherry mousse. Just like Roxy when she's rocking it onstage, it will leave you wanting plenty more.

SERVES 4

PREPARATION TIME
35 MINUTES

COOKING TIME
5 MINUTES

WHAT YOU WILL NEED

1¼ cups/7 oz/200 g milk chocolate
Finely grated zest of 1 orange
4 large eggs, separated
2½ tbsp/1 oz/30 g sugar
Scant 1 cup/7 fl oz/200 ml heavy/double cream
4 tbsp cherry jam
Handful of milk chocolate malted candies

You will need 4 serving glasses or small bowls.

1. Put the chocolate in a heat-resistant bowl and set over a pan of barely simmering water, making sure the water is not in contact with the bowl. Once melted, leave the chocolate until it's cool but still runny, then stir in the orange zest.
2. Whisk the egg yolks and sugar together until light in color. Pour in the cream and whisk until you have soft peaks. Don't overwhisk or the mousse will become heavy.
3. In a separate grease-free bowl, whisk the egg whites until very stiff.
4. Fold the cooled chocolate into the cream mixture, then gently fold in the egg whites, making sure not to beat the mixture. You want to keep as much air in it as possible.
5. Fill your glasses half full, then add a tablespoon of the cherry jam to each glass. Top with more mousse and put the glasses in the fridge to set for at least an hour.
6. Before serving, crush the milk chocolate malted candies and sprinkle the crumbs over the mousse.

Freddy Fact

If you're looking for high-speed motor mayhem, Roxy Raceway is the place to be. Sign up today and be a winner! Nobody likes a loser.

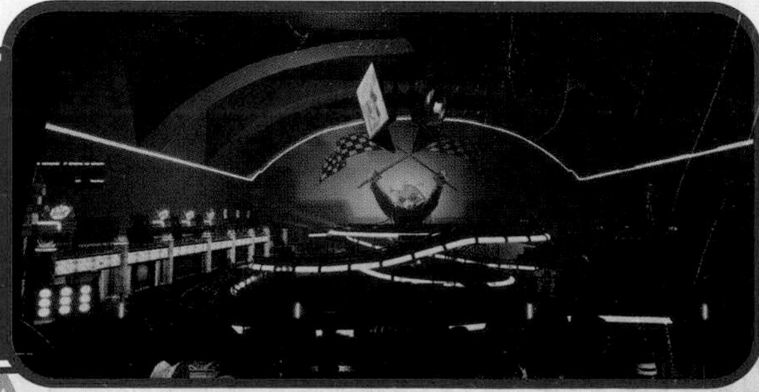

If you can get all three upgrades for Freddy and return to the Raceway, you'll find an underground passage that leads to the ruins of the original Freddy Fazbear's Pizza Place!

Freddy Fazbear's Pizza Place

Pirate Plunderbar

Endorsed by Foxy

Don't let Foxy's tattered fur and unkempt appearance fool you—he's a cunning pirate animatronic capable of conjuring a top treat. These sweet, chocolate Plunderbars can be cut into any shape, but make sure Foxy doesn't use his hook!

MAKES 9+ PLUNDERBARS

PREPARATION TIME
35 MINUTES

WHAT YOU WILL NEED

½ cup/5½ oz/150 g light corn syrup/golden syrup

⅝ cup/6 oz/175 g smooth peanut butter

5 cups/4 ¼ oz/120 g rice cereal

FOR THE TOPPING

1¼ cups/7 oz/200 g milk chocolate

2 tbsp/1 oz/25 g unsalted butter

1 cup/1 oz/25 g mini marshmallows

3 tbsp colored sprinkles

1. Grease an 8 inch/20 cm square cake pan with butter or line with parchment paper.
2. Put the syrup and peanut butter in a saucepan and melt over low heat, stirring often until you have a smooth sauce. Fold in the rice cereal, making sure all the crispies are coated with the sauce.
3. Pour the mixture into the prepared pan, press it into the pan with the back of a spoon until firm. Put in the fridge to set.
4. Place a small saucepan of water over low heat. Break the chocolate into small pieces and place into a heat-resistant bowl with the butter. Set the bowl over the hot water, making sure the water isn't in contact with the bowl. Leave to melt, then cool slightly.
5. Pour the melted cooled chocolate over the rice cereal, arrange the mini marshmallows on top, then add the sprinkles, and put back into the fridge to set.
6. Once set, remove from the pan, slice, and enjoy. But make sure you stop other pirates from plundering your delicious dessert bars!

Freddy Fudgebar

CHOCOLATE FUDGE BROWNIES

If moving through this world of animatronics and adventure begins to zap your energy, pause for a Freddy-themed brownie to boost you back up. It's a chocolate and fudge delight that's a perfect treat as you indulge in the Pizzaplex entertainment.

MAKES 12

 **PREPARATION TIME**
20 MINUTES

 **COOKING TIME**
35 MINUTES

WHAT YOU WILL NEED

- ¾ cup/6 oz/175 g unsalted butter, plus extra for greasing
- 2 chocolate, caramel, and nougat snack bars, roughly chopped
- 6¼ oz/180 g bittersweet/dark chocolate, roughly broken
- 3 large eggs
- 1¾ cups/12 oz/350 g sugar
- 1 tsp vanilla extract
- Scant 1 cup/4½ oz/125 g all-purpose flour
- 1 tsp baking powder
- Heaped ⅓ cup/1½ oz/40 g cocoa powder
- ¾ cup/3½ oz/100 g toasted hazelnuts, chopped

1. Heat the oven to 350°F/160°C/gas 4. Grease an 11 x 8 inch/28 x 20 cm baking dish and line with parchment paper.
2. Put butter, chopped snack bars, and chocolate in a heat-resistant bowl and set over a pan of barely simmering water, making sure the water is not in contact with the bowl. Stir occasionally until you have a smooth sauce, then remove from the heat.
3. In a large bowl, whisk the eggs and sugar together until light and fluffy. Fold the cooled chocolate mixture and the vanilla into the eggs. Sift in the flour, baking powder, and cocoa, then add half the hazelnuts and fold everything together.
4. Pour the batter into the prepared baking dish and sprinkle the remaining hazelnuts. Bake for 25–30 minutes until a skewer comes out almost clean—you still want it slightly gooey. Leave to cool completely before removing from the dish.
5. Slice the brownie into 12 pieces to serve. These will keep for 4–5 days in an airtight container.

Freddy Fact

The Fudgebar and the Fazbar are endorsed by Freddy. The snack bars are fine for a quick and easy munch, but they won't keep you going all night!

Sunnydrop's Energy Balls

On the flip side of Moondrop comes the welcoming rays of the Sunnydrop brand. While the Pizzaplex offers Sunnydrop Energizing Candy, these energy balls are much more fulfilling, with seeds, dates, and nuts combining for a striking snack.

MAKES 12

PREPARATION TIME
25 MINUTES

WHAT YOU WILL NEED

- 1 cup/5½ oz/150 g Medjool dates
- 1¼ cups/5½ oz/150 g nuts (walnuts, pecans, cashew, or a mix of all three)
- 2½ tbsp/⅔ oz/20 g chia seeds
- 2½ tbsp/1¾ oz/50 g pumpkin seeds
- 2½ tbsp/1 oz/25 g sunflower seeds
- ⅓ cup/1¾ oz/50 g dried cranberries
- 1 tbsp honey
- 4 tbsp cocoa powder
- 1 tsp vanilla extract
- Juice and zest of 1 orange
- 1 oz/30 g dried shredded/desiccated coconut
- 3½ oz/100 g granola
- Oil, for greasing

1. Put all the ingredients except the granola into a food processor and blend until you have a thick, sticky mixture.
2. Put the granola into a freezer bag and, using a rolling pin, crush into crumbs. Place the granola crumbs into a shallow bowl.
3. With slightly oiled hands, scoop bite-sized portions of the mixture and roll into balls. Fully coat each ball by rolling them in the crushed granola. These balls can be stored in an airtight container for up to a week.

Freddy Fact

The Sun Daycare Attendant is friendly and helpful. That's everything that Moon isn't!

good
vibes

RASPBERRY & WHITE CHOCOLATE MR. CUPCAKES

Chica and the rest of the animatronics enjoy an upgrade every now and then. These raspberry and white chocolate treats are definitely an upgrade to regular cupcakes! Googly eyes at the ready!

MAKES 12

PREPARATION TIME
40 MINUTES

COOKING TIME
25 MINUTES

WHAT YOU WILL NEED

1 cup/4¼ oz/120 g fresh raspberries

2¼ cups/10½ oz/300 g all-purpose/plain flour

1 tsp baking powder

1 cup/7 oz/200 g sugar

Pinch of salt

Scant ½ cup/3½ fl oz/100 ml sour cream

2 large eggs, beaten

Scant ½ cup/3½ fl oz/100 ml milk

Scant ½ cup/3½ fl oz/100 ml vegetable oil

1 tsp vanilla extract

⅔ cup/3½ oz/100 g white chocolate chunks

FOR THE ICING

¼ cup/1 oz/30 g fresh raspberries

1 tbsp lemon juice

½ tsp vanilla extract

1 cup/5½ oz/150 g confectioner's/icing sugar

FOR DECORATION

Edible googly eyes

1. Preheat the oven to 350°F/180°C/gas 5 and, if you don't have a nonstick muffin tin, grease a 12-hole muffin pan.
2. Place the raspberries in a bowl, add 1 tablespoon of the flour, and toss so the raspberries are coated in the flour. Set aside.
3. Sift the rest of the flour and the baking powder into a mixing bowl and add the sugar and salt.
4. In a separate bowl, whisk together the sour cream, eggs, milk, vegetable oil, and vanilla extract. Pour the milky egg mixture into the flour and mix until you have a smooth batter. Gently fold in the raspberries and white chocolate.
5. Divide the mixture between the holes of the muffin pan. Bake for 20–25 minutes until risen and golden. Leave to cool completely in the pan before removing.
6. While the muffins are cooling, make the icing. Press the raspberries through a fine mesh strainer/sieve into a bowl, discarding the bits. Stir in the lemon juice and vanilla. Add half the confectioner's sugar and stir until fully incorporated. Add the rest of the sugar slowly, a tablespoon at a time, until you have the consistency you want.
7. Once the cakes are cool, spoon a tablespoon of the icing over each one, letting it drip down the sides. Leave the icing to set for 10 minutes before adding googly eyes.

Dancing Rabbit Lady's SIZZLING CHURROS

Dancing Rabbit Lady—aka Vanny—enjoys skipping and shuffling in pursuit of young Gregory. She's a bunny not to be messed with! Time to swap the frightening for the frying, though, with sizzling churros served with easy chocolate sauce!

MAKES ABOUT 15

PREPARATION TIME
20 MINUTES

COOKING TIME
30 MINUTES

WHAT YOU WILL NEED

½ cup/4 fl oz/125 ml whole milk
2 tbsp/1 oz/30 g butter
1 tbsp sugar
Pinch of salt
1 tsp vanilla extract
1 cup plus 2 tbsp/5½ oz/150 g all-purpose/plain flour
2 large eggs
Vegetable or sunflower oil, for frying

FOR THE COATING

1 tbsp sugar
1 tsp ground cinnamon

FOR THE EASY CHOCOLATE SAUCE (optional)

½ cup/4 fl oz/125 ml heavy/double cream
2 tbsp/1 oz/25 g butter
1 tbsp sugar
¼ cup/1¾ oz/50 g dark chocolate

You will need a piping bag fitted with a star-shaped tip/nozzle and a pair of scissors.

1. Put the milk, butter, sugar, and salt into a saucepan and gently heat. Add the vanilla and bring to a boil. Remove the pan from the heat and beat in the flour with a wooden spoon until you have a lump-free dough. Cool for 15 minutes.
2. While the mixture is cooling, make the chocolate sauce, if you're using. Put the heavy cream, butter, and sugar into a saucepan and gently heat. Place the chocolate into a microwavable bowl and heat in 5 second increments until melted. Remove the cream from the heat and stir in the melted chocolate to make a smooth sauce.
3. Combine the sugar and cinnamon for coating in a bowl and set aside.
4. Once the batter has cooled, beat in the eggs, making sure they are fully incorporated. Spoon the thick dough into a piping bag fitted with a star tip/nozzle.
5. Pour the oil into a heavy deep-sided pan to a depth of about 2 inches/5 cm. Using a kitchen thermometer, heat the oil to 350°F/180°C. You can also do this in a deep fryer.
6. Pipe the batter straight into the hot oil and, as you pipe, use scissors to snip through the dough at roughly 4-inch/10-cm intervals to create the churros. Cook a few at a time, frying each batch for about 2 minutes, and turning over after a minute, until they are golden and crisp. Remove the churros from the oil with a slotted spoon and drain onto paper towels/kitchen roll, then toss in the cinnamon sugar to coat.
7. Eat while hot and serve with the warm chocolate sauce, if you are using.

Rock & Roll

13

Montgomery Gator's

BEVERAGES

Running around the Pizzaplex arcade is definitely thirsty work. While animatronics rarely stop for liquid refueling, human visitors need hydration of the highest order. Cans of Sodaroni (a weird pepperoni-flavored drink) can be spotted everywhere, but a more sophisticated and enjoyable selection of beverages are about to be revealed. Cheers!

Monty Gator's

GREEN WITH ENVY!

With his glamrock attitude and star-shaped sunglasses, Monty Gator makes a healthy smoothie that puts all other Pizzaplex drinks in the shade. It's speedy to make, so use your spare time for a quick game of Gator Golf!

SERVES 2

PREPARATION TIME
10 MINUTES

WHAT YOU WILL NEED

- 1 apple, cored
- 1 banana, peeled
- 1 tsp grated fresh ginger
- Small handful of spinach
- Small handful of kale
- 1 tbsp chia seeds
- ¼ cucumber
- 15 mint leaves
- Juice of 2 limes
- 3 ice cubes
- Scant 1 cup/7 oz/200 ml apple juice, plus extra if needed
- 1 tbsp honey

1. Place all ingredients into a blender and blend until smooth.
2. If it feels thick, add more apple juice. Serve right away. This is certainly a boost you need first thing in the morning.

Monty Mystery Mix is a strange green pizza-topping gloop, which can be used to lure—and finally destroy—Chica. Mean and green!

MONTGOMERY
GATOR

SUPERSTAR DAYCARE Strawberry Shake

Fancy a trip to Superstar Daycare? It's a big adventure soft-play area full of stuff to slide down, climb over, and explore. Mix up a strawberry-flavored Superstar Daycare shake to experience your own mouthwatering fun!

SERVES 2

PREPARATION TIME
5 MINUTES

WHAT YOU WILL NEED

1½ cups/9 oz/250 g strawberries, sliced

1 tsp sugar

1¼ cups/10 fl oz/300 ml milk, plus extra if needed

2 scoops vanilla ice cream

1 tbsp chia seeds

TO SERVE (optional)

Scant ½ cup/3½ fl oz/100 ml whipping cream

1 tsp colored sprinkles

1. Put the sliced strawberries into a bowl with the sugar, mix, and let soften for 15 minutes.
2. Put the strawberries into a blender and add the milk, ice cream, and chia seeds. Blend until smooth, adding a little more milk if it's too thick.
3. Serve in two chilled glasses, topped with whipped cream and colored sprinkles if you are using.

Keep clear of the flashlight-tastic security bots around Superstar Daycare. These machines are 100 percent party poopers.

Foxy's
FRUITY COVE COOLER

The action in Foxy's Pirate Cove can get a little heated, so it makes sense to help turn the temperature down with a fruity cooler drink! Grab some pineapple, passion fruit, and plenty of ice to create a glass of something that's rewarding and refreshing.

SERVES 2

PREPARATION TIME
10 MINUTES

WHAT YOU WILL NEED

1 small pineapple, skin removed and flesh chopped

1¼ cups/10 fl oz/300 ml coconut water

2 passion fruits

Juice of 1 lime

1 tbsp honey

¼ cup/1¾ oz/50 g ice, plus extra to serve

TO GARNISH

10 mint sprigs

Lime wedges

1. Put the prepared pineapple, coconut water, passion fruit pulp, lime juice, honey, and ice into a blender. Blend on full power until you have a smooth drink.
2. Take two long glasses and add a few ice cubes to each. Pour the cooler into the glasses and stir in the mint sprigs and a couple of lime wedges.

EST. 1986

SODARONI Slushy

Unlike retail cans of Sodaroni, which have the strange taste of pepperoni, your homemade Sodaroni in a tall glass is a flash of flavorsome fruitiness. Whatever fruit you pick to make it, you'll lap up the icy goodness of this simple but stylish slushy.

SERVES 2

PREPARATION TIME
5 MINUTES

WHAT YOU WILL NEED

9 oz/250 g frozen raspberries

Juice of 1 large lemon

Scant ½ cup/3½ fl oz/100 ml sparkling water

Scant ½ cup/3½ fl oz/100 ml cranberry juice

¾ cup/5½ oz/150 g ice

1 tbsp honey

1. Put all the ingredients in a blender and blend until smooth and slushy.
2. Pour into two glasses and enjoy.

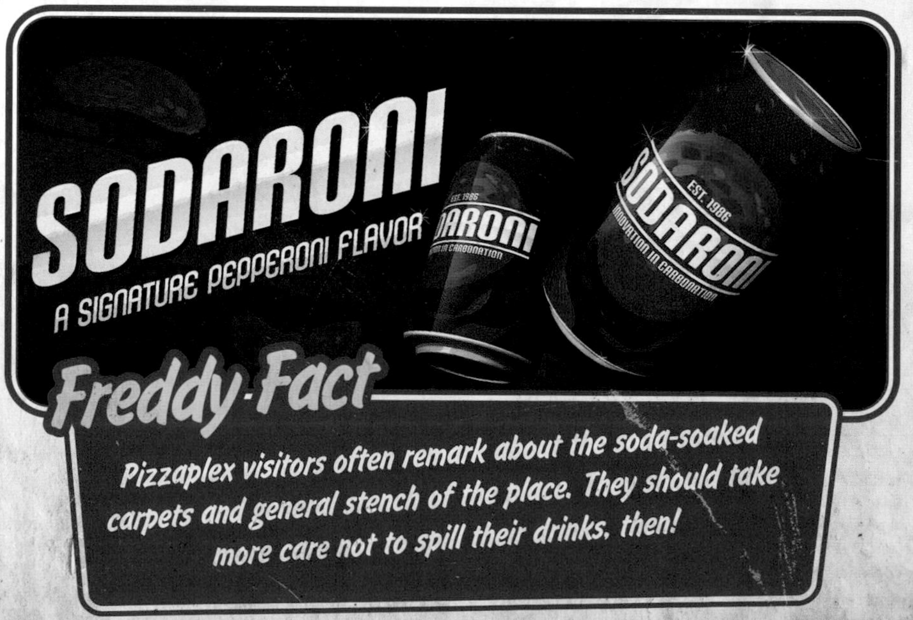

Freddy Fact

Pizzaplex visitors often remark about the soda-soaked carpets and general stench of the place. They should take more care not to spill their drinks, then!

Freddy's Top Tips!
★ You could replace the raspberries here with strawberries, blackberries, or a mix of berries—just make sure they are frozen.

Monty's Mouthwatering MELON MELTDOWN

Show that you have a smooth side, too, by serving up this marvelous fruity mocktail. The watermelon, mint, lime, honey, and soda combo comes together perfectly for quite a unique taste. Top work!

MAKES 2

PREPARATION TIME
10 MINUTES

WHAT YOU WILL NEED

¾ cup/7 oz/200 g watermelon, seeds removed

1 tbsp honey

5 mint leaves

Juice of 2 limes

1¼ cups/10 fl oz/300 ml soda water, chilled

TO SERVE

Ice, for the glasses

2 tbsp grenadine (optional)

Extra mint leaves

2 slices lime

2 small watermelon wedges

1. Put the watermelon in a blender with the honey, mint leaves, and lime juice and blend until smooth. Add the soda water and blend for another couple seconds.
2. Add ice to two tall glasses, top with the watermelon drink, and pour in the grenadine, if using. Garnish each glass with mint leaves, a watermelon wedge, and a slice of lime. Serve immediately.

Freddy Fact

Don't forget to visit Monty's Gator Golf (aka Monty Golf and formerly Monty's Wild Golf). Home of the Hurricane Hole-in-One!

Index

COMING SOON!

Fazbear's Fright: The Horror Attraction!

Local amusement park is getting ready to scare your socks off with a new attraction based on the unsolved mysteries of Freddy Fazbear's Pizza.

Featuring actual relics from the decades-old pizzeria, this new attraction is guaranteed to bring back your childhood in the worst possible way.

IT BURNS!

Fazbear's Fright burns to the ground!

A new local attraction based on an ancient pizzeria chain burned down overnight.

Authorities have not ruled out foul play, but at the moment it seems to have been caused by faulty wiring.

Very little was found at the scene. The few items that were salvaged will be sold at public auction.

COME BACK
REAL SOON!